SECTION 60
ARLINGTON NATIONAL CEMETERY

On Hallowed Ground:
The Story of Arlington National Cemetery

Explorers House:
National Geographic and the World It Made

SECTION 60

ARLINGTON NATIONAL CEMETERY

WHERE WAR COMES HOME

★ ★ ★

ROBERT M. POOLE

B L O O M S B U R Y

NEW YORK · LONDON · OXFORD · NEW DELHI · SYDNEY

Bloomsbury USA
An imprint of Bloomsbury Publishing Plc

1385 Broadway	50 Bedford Square
New York	London
NY 10018	WC1B 3DP
USA	UK

www.bloomsbury.com

First published 2014
This paperback edition published 2015

ISBN: HB: 978-1-62040-293-1
PB: 978-1-62040-295-5
ePub: 978-1-62040-294-8

Library of Congress Cataloging-in-Publication Data

Poole, Robert M.
Section 60 : Arlington National Cemetery : where
war comes home / Robert M. Poole.
pages cm
Includes bibliographical references and index.
ISBN: 978-1-62040-293-1 (alk. paper)
1. Arlington National Cemetery (Arlington, Va.)—History—21st century.
2. Families of military personnel—United States. 3. Memorial Day. 4.
Afghan War, 2001—Casualties—United States. 5. Iraq War, 2003–2011—
Casualties—United States. I. Title. II. Title: Section 60, Arlington National
Cemetery. III. Title: Arlington National Cemetery, where war comes home.
F234.A7P67 2014
975.5'295—dc23
2014017528

Printed an...   ...Michigan

To find out m...   ...m. Here you
will find extracts, a...   ...option to sign

Bloomsbury bo...   ...or information
on bulk purchases...   ...Department at

CONTENTS

People die only when we forget them . . .

—Isabel Allende, *Eva Luna*

Tombs form ranks in Section 60. (Bruce Dale)

ARLINGTON NATIONAL CEMETERY

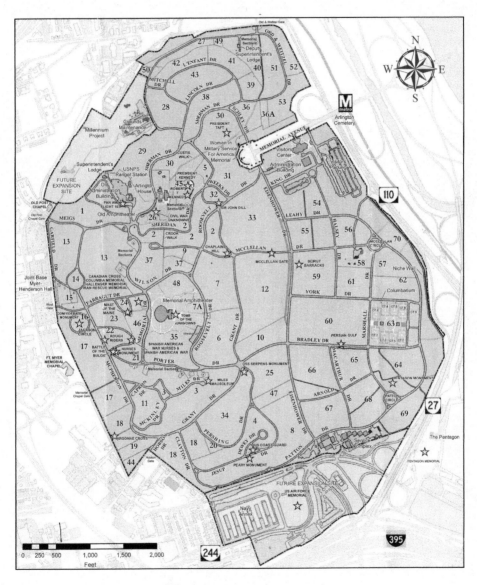

(Arlington National Cemetery)

1

THE LONGEST WAR

FOR MOST OF the country, the longest war in the history of the United States has taken place largely out of sight, the casualties piling up in faraway Iraq and Afghanistan while normal life continued on the home front, with no war taxes, no draft notices, no gas rationing, and none of the shared sacrifice of the nation's earlier conflicts.

The one exception has been in Section 60, a corner of Arlington National Cemetery where more than nine hundred men and women have come to rest in the past decade. "This is one of the few places you'd know we've had a war going on," said retired Navy Cdr. Kirk S. Lippold, who stood near the center of Section 60 on a fine May morning as cemetery workers tidied the graves and rolled out plush new mats of turf in preparation for another Memorial Day.[1]

Lippold, former skipper of the *USS Cole*, had come to pay his respects to three shipmates, Technician Second Class

Kenneth Eugene Clodfelter, Chief Petty Officer Richard Dean Costlow, and Seaman Cherone Louis Gunn, now lying side by side beneath neat white tombstones. Months before the phrase "9/11" entered the language, this trio of sailors became early casualties in the long war, killed on October 12, 2000, after two suicide bombers from Al Qaeda approached the *Cole*, detonated explosives packed in their motorboat, and almost succeeded in sinking the 8,400-ton guided-missile destroyer while it was refueling in Yemen. Along with Clodfelter, Costlow, and Gunn, fourteen other sailors died in the explosion, which might be considered the opening shot of a conflict now known as the Global War on Terror.[2]

"Their deaths were prelude to everything that's happened in Iraq and Afghanistan," said Lippold. "It was an act of war, no doubt about that." As he spoke, a few other pilgrims wandered the cemetery, bringing fresh carnations and roses to nearby tombstones, spreading blankets on graves, and resuming their conversations with the dead. Before long hundreds of

Bordered by streets named for famous soldiers, Section 60 has added hundreds of graves from recent wars. (Robert M. Poole)

Friends and relatives bring offerings of flowers and beer for a soldier.
(Bruce Dale)

soldiers from nearby Fort Myer would swarm among the headstones to plant miniature American flags at each grave for Memorial Day, a spring ritual of remembrance with roots in the Civil War.[3]

In the years since the *Cole* bombing, Section 60 has been busy, with the crack of rifle salutes and the silvery notes of Taps announcing the arrival of new conscripts with depressing frequency—several times a day at the peak of the recent wars. The most active subdivision of Arlington, Section 60 occupies just fourteen acres of the 624-acre cemetery, but this postage stamp of earth represents something much larger. It is a place to mourn those lost in America's latest war, to remember each of those sacrificed, and to recount the journeys that brought them here, a place to consider how their wartime experience compares with that of those who fought in World War II, Korea, and Vietnam, all of whom share space in Section 60.

The whole history of our recent wars can be traced among the closely packed tombstones, which mark the graves of soldiers, sailors, marines, and airmen, each of whom earned a berth at Arlington by volunteering, suiting up, and paying the ultimate sacrifice in Iraq or Afghanistan. Many came home in pieces, dismembered by the signature weapons of our latest conflict—suicide bombs and improvised explosive devices (IEDs), which often cheated families out of the age-old ritual of seeing brothers, fathers, sons, and daughters one last time. Other warriors came to Section 60 as the result of storybook bravery, instinctively throwing themselves on grenades, fatally walking point on foot patrol, leading the charge into enemy strongholds, or drowning while trying to save comrades struggling in canals and rivers. Quite a few were shot by snipers, while others were knocked from the sky in hostile territory, killed in airplane or chopper accidents, or gunned down in

A caisson team plods by Section 60 after a funeral. (Bruce Dale)

sneak attacks—the all too familiar "green on blue" killings of recent years—at the hands of supposed Afghan allies. A handful of the toughest and the bravest survived frequent combat deployments, came home, and tried to settle into civilian life, only to falter from depression, post-traumatic stress disorder (PTSD), or other invisible injuries that consigned them to Arlington.

Those buried in Section 60 achieve a kind of immortality as friends, family, and comrades converge on this part of Arlington to keep their memories alive. The living come to remember birthdays, celebrate anniversaries, and recall exploits from "downrange," as combatants refer to the battlefront these days. Most visits include a gift or memento to show that someone still cares. Kids bring report cards for parental review, wives bring sonograms of unborn children, fiancés come with love letters. Comrades who were present at a friend's death leave a quarter to commemorate the moment, or a penny to show they were in boot camp together. Some of

Well-wishers crowd Section 60 on Memorial Day and other holidays, setting up camp and passing hours there. (Robert M. Poole)

these tributes are left to fade in the rain and humidity; others are written on rocks in indelible ink. "I thank you for coming into my life & changing it," read one of the latter, left for Army Pfc. Jalfred Vaquerano, killed in Afghanistan. "Thank you for loving me until the end . . . I will see you soon my love."[4] A two-year-old named Christian, dressed head to toe in camouflage for Memorial Day, ran over to his father's grave, patted the stone, and shouted: "Bye-bye, Daddy! I love you."[5]

Anthony Coyer, having made the long overnight drive from Saginaw, Michigan, with his wife and daughter, set up lawn chairs before his son Ryan's tombstone in Section 60, and shared a few toasts of Jack Daniel's with the dead Army Ranger, who was twenty-six when he died. Tony fell asleep in the warm spring sunlight, napping companionably on his son's grave.[6] Beth Belle brought little flags and fresh flowers for her son, Marine Lance Cpl. Nicholas C. Kirven, twenty-one. Peeking into a white bakery box someone had left for him, she expressed approval. "Oh, he loved sugar cookies!" she said, easing the box back onto the grass in front of Grave No. 60-8180.[7] Paula Davis released a cloud of yellow balloons and sang Happy Birthday to her only son, Army Pfc. Justin R. Davis, who was nineteen when he was killed. "He'd be old enough to drink by now."[8]

Marine Lance Cpl. Brandon Long, who lost his legs in Afghanistan, wheeled over the turf, stopped at the tombstone of Cpl. Derek Allen Wyatt, and lit two Newports, one for himself and one for his buddy. Leaning over the edge of his wheelchair, Long tenderly placed Wyatt's cigarette in the grass like a joss stick and watched the smoke coil toward the sky. "He never bought one for himself but always expected one from me," Long said with a tight smile.[9] Master Sgt. David V. Hill, a former Green Beret with numerous deployments to Iraq and Afghanistan, halted before the grave of Army Maj. Jeffrey P. Toczylowski, known to his friends as Toz, and broke

Lance Cpl. Brandon Long shares a smoke at a fellow Marine's grave in Section 60. (Robert M. Poole)

into a smile, recalling the dead man's memorable—and generous—parting gesture.[10]

"He fell out of a chopper in Iraq," said Hill. "That's what killed him." A few days later Toz's friends and family received an e-mail from the dead Special Forces officer: "If you are getting this e-mail, it means that I have passed away," Toz wrote. "No, it's not a sick Toz joke, but a letter I wanted to write in case this happened." He invited recipients to his service at Arlington "but I understand if you can't make it. There will also be a party in Vegas," he wrote, announcing that he had set aside $100,000 to cover travel, rooms, and other expenses for those attending his farewell bash. A year later more than a hundred friends converged on the Palms Hotel and Casino, where Toz's mother, Peggy, greeted well-wishers, sparsely dressed barmaids served liquor from an open bar, and a disc jockey ramped up the music. A life-sized cardboard cutout of Major Toczylowski presided over the all-night party, which included a limbo contest and photo ops with Toz's stand-in.[11]

"I wish I had been there!" said Hill, who was overseas at the time. "I heard it was some party."[12]

Few others have left the stage with Toz's flair. But all are remembered and sorely missed by those who flock to Section 60, now almost full after a dozen years of conflict. Until something replaces it, this part of Arlington will serve as a memorial for the recent wars, a point of contact for the community of the living and the community of the dead. Their stories are the subject of this book, which is a heartfelt salute to those on both sides of the grave.

2

RANGERS LEAD THE WAY

D URING TWO COMBAT tours in Vietnam, first as a captain then as a major, Joe Rippetoe constantly worried about the perils of operating in a war zone. But the hardest mission he ever faced came long after the retired lieutenant colonel's fighting days were finished. It was April 10, 2003, a raw spring morning with damp winds scattering the cherry blossoms in Washington, D.C., as Rippetoe, sixty-six, got into his old dress green uniform, made sure the creases were sharp and the ribbons perfectly aligned, and headed for Section 60 of Arlington National Cemetery.[1]

There, accompanied by his wife, Rita, and more than 150 well-wishers, he would watch his only son, Army Capt. Russell Brian Rippetoe, twenty-seven, committed to the earth, the first combat casualty of the Iraq War to be buried at Arlington. The younger Rippetoe, an elite Army Ranger like his father, had fulfilled the unit's motto, "Rangers Lead the Way!" twice over—first by parachuting into Iraq as the war opened, then by pioneering the path to Section 60, where more than nine hundred fellow service members would join him from Iraq and Afghanistan in the decade following his burial.[2]

The elder Rippetoe, sitting rigid in the front row at graveside, grimaced and fought back tears as the solemn honors ran their course: six matched gray horses in gleaming tack delivered the flag-draped casket, escorted by Rangers in their distinctive tan berets and polished paratrooper boots; a white-haired Army chaplain in dress blues read from Scripture; the Army band, Pershing's Own, lined up on the green turf to render a slow, sweet version of "The Battle Hymn of the Republic"; wounded comrades from the dead captain's company left their beds at Walter Reed Army Medical Center to pay tribute; a firing party from the Old Guard uncorked a flawless three-rifle salute; and while the scent of gun smoke still hung in the air, a bugler, standing all alone among the tombstones, lifted his instrument and sent the sound of Taps spilling over the cemetery, last stop on a young soldier's all-too-brief journey.[3]

Joe Rippetoe, disabled from his Vietnam service, struggled to stand and gripped his right wrist with his strong left hand, guiding his weaker arm into position for a final salute to the boy he knew as Rusty, with whom he had been particularly close.[4] Just before Russell's final deployment, Joe had showered him with hard-won advice. "Never handle a body, yours or theirs, unless you see it fall in front of you," he wrote, signing his memo Ranger Rip Senior. "Keep weapons and feet in excellent condition, all else will follow . . . Make every shot count . . . When you have nothing to do, dig a deeper hole, rest, eat, ready weapon, study map . . . Don't wait to introduce yourself to the Lord, get to know him now. In combat you want to be on a first name basis."[5]

The son rose through the ranks, absorbed the old man's lessons, and went off to war, first to Afghanistan, then to Iraq.

He carried his father's battered combat knife from Vietnam, along with dog tags inscribed with the warrior's credo from Joshua 1:9: "Be strong and courageous. Do not be afraid. Do not be discouraged, for the Lord your God will be with you wherever you go."[6]

Years later, in an upstairs room of the family's home in Gaithersburg, Maryland, surrounded by pictures of his son, combat maps, folded flags, and other memorabilia, Rippetoe flipped through the pages of Russell's war journal. Hanging on the back of a door within easy reach were two neatly pressed sets of battle fatigues, one for the father (green and brown cammies from the Vietnam era), one for the son (pixelated tan battle dress uniform for desert fighting), both ready for sudden deployment. "The new ones are much better," said Joe, absently fingering his son's sleeve and recalling the last time they had spoken, on March 8, 2003. "That was the day before he left for Iraq. He called me four times and didn't say much of anything. It was like he was worried but didn't know what

Capt. Russell B. Rippetoe, between deployments to Afghanistan and Iraq.
(Joe Rippetoe)

to say," said Rippetoe. "The fourth time he called, he said, 'Dad, I'll call you when I get back. I leave in ten minutes.' Like a dummy, I couldn't figure out why he kept calling. I wish I had told him I loved him."[7]

As a veteran with twenty-eight years of service, the elder Rippetoe has lived through every phase of war, on the front lines as well as the home front. "I've been through the whole cycle," he said. "I was the guy in combat, the one who went to take care of families as a casualty officer, the one waiting for calls and letters at home—and now I've buried my son." Joe knew the dangers Russell would face in Iraq, just as he knew exactly why the doorbell started ringing in the wee hours of April 3, 2003. Both Rippetoes straggled out of bed and shuffled down the stairs to find three Rangers on their doorstep. Opening the door, Joe tried to reassure the young soldiers who had turned out to comfort him. "You don't have to say anything," said Joe, remembering the times he had made such late-night calls. "I've done what you're doing."[8]

He invited the soldiers in. They gave their report, sketching out how Russell had been killed by suicide bombers northwest of Baghdad, just as the first wave of allied troops rolled into the Iraqi capital. Soldiers from Rippetoe's unit, the Third Battalion of the 75th Ranger Regiment, parachuted into an abandoned airport in western Iraq, secured it, and moved on to take control of the strategically important Haditha Dam on the Euphrates River. Rippetoe's Alpha Company peeled off to establish roadblocks near the Syrian border, where they hoped to intercept fleeing members of Saddam Hussein's ruling Ba'athist regime.[9]

And it was there, said Joe Rippetoe, that his son's big heart got him killed.[10]

Army Capt. Chad Thibodeau, who had been a young specialist working the checkpoint with Russell Rippetoe, explained what happened. "Lots of people were trying to get out," said Thibodeau. "If you saw an old van with seven kids and ma and grandma and basically everything they can pack into their vehicle, we let them go. They were just trying to get away from the action. But if it was a new Mercedes or a Suburban with just a couple of people in it, that raised a red flag. We'd stop those for further questioning."[11]

Comrades near Haditha radioed Thibodeau that just such a vehicle was approaching their roadblock in the predawn hours of April 3. He and other Rangers stopped the car, the front passenger door flew open, and an agitated woman jumped out, waving her arms around. "We're hungry!" she screamed. "We're thirsty!"[12]

The woman, who in some reports appeared to be pregnant, created such a commotion that it attracted the attention of Rippetoe, who had been huddling with another officer at a temporary command post some distance away.[13] "He came down to find out what was going on," said Thibodeau. "That was absolutely within Russ's personality. If he thought somebody was in trouble, he was going to help. He felt for this woman. He told me to go up the hill and get half a case of water and some MREs [Meals Ready to Eat] for her. So that's what I did. I collected the stuff and was coming back. I got within ten feet of the vehicle, and that's when it blew up. There was a tremendous flash."[14]

The blast, from a suicide bomb thought to be in the car, lifted the vehicle more than forty feet in the air, knocked Thibodeau flat, and sent shards of shredded metal knifing in every direction, hitting Thibodeau, Rippetoe, and three other Rangers—Staff Sgt. Nino D. Livaudais, Spec. Ryan P. Long, and Spec. Kyle S. Smith. The car's male driver and the woman were killed. A second woman, whom Thibodeau had seen in the back seat, was killed. Rippetoe, Livaudais, and Long died on the spot, while Kyle Smith and Thibodeau, situated farther away, survived the explosion.[15]

"I wake up and I'm facedown in the dirt," recalled Thibodeau, who took shrapnel to his face, eyes, and stomach, suffered flash burns to his face, and had both eardrums blown out; one piece of flying metal sliced through his large intestine, chopping off almost an inch at its end.[16]

"I thought to myself, *I can't believe I'm going to die in this shithole desert from a suicide bomber!*" Thibodeau recalled. "Then I thought, *Well, at least my wife will be taken care of.* I had an Army insurance policy, which paid $250,000 if I died. Then as I lay there a couple of seconds, I thought, *I'm not dead yet! I can't see anything. I can't hear anything.*"[17]

With one hand he reached up to check his eyes, which had popped out of their sockets. "They were about out to here," he said, holding his hand a half-inch in front of his face. "I looked like that character from *The Fly*." A sergeant dragged Thibodeau to a casualty collection point, where soldiers frantically tried to revive Rippetoe and the others. Medevac helicopters swarmed in. "Russ was loaded right next to me on the bird. I knew it was bad. And I heard them working on Russ, and that was the last thing I remember. They shot me up with morphine or something for the pain."[18]

Within hours of the blast at Haditha, as Thibodeau and the others were whisked away for treatment, the Arabic-language network Al Jazeera broadcast videotapes from two women claiming credit for the attack. One of the women, with an automatic rifle in one hand and a Koran in the other, identified herself as "the martyrdom-seeker Nour Qaddour al-Shammari" and a follower of "the hero commander Saddam Hussein." The other woman, who called herself Wadad Jamil Jassem, said she was devoted to "jihad for the sake of God and against the American, British, and Israeli infidels and to defend the soil of our precious and dear country." The Iraqi flag served as backdrop for both videos, suggesting that the attackers had been motivated by some strain of nationalist—or at least Ba'athist—sentiment.[19] Whatever prompted it, the bombing was an early sign that American political leaders had woefully misjudged the situation in Iraq; instead of being greeted as liberators, as Vice President Richard B. Cheney had confidently predicted on the eve of invasion, American troops were met with deadly force, a state of affairs that would prolong the conflict for years.[20]

In the days after the attack, Thibodeau drifted in and out of a haze, enduring a series of surgeries and passing through military hospitals in Kuwait, Germany, and Texas before landing for extended treatment at Walter Reed. At one point in this odyssey, he asked a nurse for a mirror to assess the damage to his face. She stalled him. *Man, that's probably not a good sign*, he thought. At another point, buddies from Alpha Company came by to deliver the news that Rippetoe, Long, and Livaudais were dead. "I know. I know," said Thibodeau. He was still mourning their loss and awaiting yet another surgery when a fellow Ranger showed up to tell him about Rippetoe's funeral.[21]

"Hey, they're burying Russ tomorrow," said First Sgt. Dennis Smith, severely injured when he parachuted into Iraq and still limping in a heavy leg brace.

"You want to go?" asked Smith, who like Thibodeau was awaiting more surgery at Walter Reed.

"Yeah, I want to go," said Thibodeau, temporarily blind in one eye, largely deaf, and slit open from ribcage to pelvis so his wounds could breathe. "Absolutely I want to go."

"I talked to the docs," said Smith. "They're not technically supposed to let you leave, but we'll see what we can do."

Next morning Smith came sweeping into Thibodeau's room with a wheelchair.

"All right, hop in."

With no uniform to wear, Thibodeau was outfitted by the Red Cross in oversize blue pants, a sweatshirt, and hiking boots. With their daughter Rebecca Kim, Joe and Rita Rippetoe met him at Arlington's Administration Building, near the cemetery

Chad Thibodeau, then an Army specialist severely wounded in the opening phase of the Iraq War, limps to a service for Capt. Russell Rippetoe in Section 60. (75th Ranger Regiment)

entrance, folded his wheelchair into their car, and gave him a lift to Section 60.

Thibodeau, feeling guilty for surviving, said little. The Rippetoes tried to reassure him. "We consider you our son now," said Rita. "You have another set of parents. Joe and I will be watching you."

As Thibodeau emerged for the service in Section 60, the Rippetoes' son-in-law Tom Kim draped his own raincoat over the injured soldier to shield him from the chill. Thibodeau looks gaunt and haunted in pictures from that day, with one eye squinting, an arm heavily bandaged, and a week's worth of stubble masking his face. "I couldn't shave because I still had shrapnel," he recalled. "I looked like a bum." This impression was underscored when Thibodeau's wheelchair got mired in the mud and he staggered to his feet, assisted by other soldiers. "I couldn't stand straight because it stretched the skin on my stomach, which was still open and really painful. So I walked hunched over, crying and blubbering through the whole thing. I was an emotional wreck."[22]

He sat with Rippetoe's family through most of the service but managed to stand as the final volley was fired. He saw the flag folded into a tight blue triangle and watched the colors pass into the hands of Rippetoe's parents, who led the way for the others who would repeat the farewell ritual time and again in the years ahead.

For Joe Rippetoe, Russell's placement at Arlington was both noble and fitting, the right home for a soldier who had loved being a Ranger and done his job with distinction. His parents, honoring his wish for a military funeral, were deeply impressed by the send-off he received at Arlington.

"If someone walked in off the street, you would've thought he was the president of the United States," said Rita. "I couldn't believe that was my baby, my son."[23]

"I am so proud today," said Joe as the crowd drifted away

Farewell for a Ranger: Sgt. First Class James MacKenzie sounds Taps for Capt. Russell Rippetoe, first casualty of the Iraq War to be buried at Arlington.
(Charles Dharapak, Associated Press)

Rita and Joe Rippetoe, with their daughter Rebecca Kim, receive medals at the funeral of their son, Capt. Russell Rippetoe.
(Getty Images: Chuck Kennedy, Knight-Ridder)

and the ground crew patiently waited to fill his son's grave. "Rusty would have been pleased."[24]

The dead live on in countless ways, their names—and sometimes their faces—persisting in tattoos; on car decals and T-shirts; in memorial golf tournaments, charitable foundations, and marathons; and on dog tags and memory bracelets worn next to the skin. Children and dogs, named for dead warriors, carry them into the future.

The day before he jumped into Iraq for the first and last time, Russell Rippetoe sensed the historic significance of his mission. "I'm having chest pains," he confided to his diary on March 27, 2003. "I think it is just from all the excitement . . . Well, it should definitely go down in the history books."[25]

Because he was the first fatality from Iraq to arrive at Arlington, Rippetoe's role in the conflict has been thoroughly documented. He will be known to millions of visitors who see his photograph and charred dog tags on display in *The Price of Freedom: Americans at War*, an exhibit at the Smithsonian's National Museum of American History, which tracks all American wars since the Revolution. He was the inspiration for a fifteen-hundred-mile motorcycle journey completed in 2004 by Tom Kim, his brother-in-law, and Matt Minnick, a fellow soldier. On an itinerary that took them from Fort Benning, Georgia, to Denver over several days, Kim piloted Rippetoe's Harley-Davidson Fat Boy, completing a road trip Rippetoe had eagerly planned for his own homecoming from Iraq. Since he could not make the journey, his friends did it for him.

Russell's memory is also preserved by fellow Rangers, who award a bronzed combat boot in his name to the winners of an annual road march at Fort Benning, where soldiers carry sixty-five pounds of equipment over eighteen to twenty-five miles in one day, competing for the best time.[26]

"We dedicate this trophy in his memory," said Col. William G. Kidd, commander of the Ranger Training Brigade, "so others can use him as a role model . . . so others can follow in his footsteps."[27]

One such Ranger is Chad Thibodeau, who has recovered most of his sight and hearing, survived a second tour of Iraq unscathed, and persevered in his Army career. Rising from the lowly rank of specialist, he now wears captain's bars, thanks in part to the encouragement and example of Russell Rippetoe, who pulled Thibodeau aside one day and urged him to apply for Officers Candidate School. "He pushed me. He set the standards. And he saved my life. I think of him every day," said Thibodeau, now assigned to the Army's Human Resources Command at Fort Knox, Kentucky.[28]

"I honestly believe that the reason I'm here today is that Russ and Nino and Ryan were between myself and the vehicle. Had I not been coming back from grabbing that stuff Russ wanted, I would've been closer to the bomb. So I live."

And so does Gunnar Harley Brian Thibodeau, a son born to Chad and Fawn Thibodeau a year after Rippetoe's death. "The Brian is from Russ's middle name," said Thibodeau, "our way of honoring my friend."

Gunnar, a self-contained boy with blue eyes and blond shoulder-length hair, sat quietly through his father's long interview in a Louisville hotel room, listening to war stories while thumbing a computer game at high speed.

"Hey," the interviewer asked, "are you going to follow the old man into the Army?"

"I'm going to follow him into the Rangers, and then I'm going to be in Special Operations, Delta Force," said Gunnar.

"And what about college?"

"West Point," he said, calmly returning to the computer.[29]

★   ★   ★

Russell Rippetoe's grave lies at the heart of Section 60, a neat green rectangle bounded by tree-lined streets named for famous soldiers—Eisenhower, York, Marshall, and Bradley. It is relatively flat land, so close to the Potomac River that on some days an east wind carries the fecund scent of black mud and good fishing over the tombstones. Ospreys and cormorants patrol the river, occasionally snatching a bass or shad from the current and flapping away with it.

Except for wilting humidity in summer and numbing winds in winter, nature seldom intrudes on the decorum of Section 60. Canada geese commute daily from river to cemetery, sometimes performing flyovers and honking in formation as if they are part of the ceremony. When the crack of rifles announces the end of a funeral, visitors almost always flinch at the sound, but not the geese. Accustomed to the racket, they continue calmly grazing, their somber gray plumage entirely in harmony with the surroundings.

Years before this part of Arlington was planted with tombstones, it supported a succession of living communities, from the time of Native American occupation until the arrival in 1608 of Capt. John Smith. The English explorer called local Indians the Patawomeke, which was also the name he assigned to their river. It was so thick with fish, Smith wrote, that "we attempted to catch them with a frying pan."[30] In succeeding years, the land was surveyed and parceled into large riverside holdings, including an eleven-hundred-acre piece inherited in 1799 by George Washington Parke Custis, grandson of Martha Washington and adopted son of George Washington. Largely undeveloped when Custis took ownership, the property contained wooded hills, rich bottomlands, and a few scattered shacks. Using his slaves to do the work, Custis began constructing an imposing Greek Revival mansion in 1802, just as the nation's new capital took shape across the river. He required sixteen years to finish his home, which came to be known as

Arlington House, named for the family's ancestral estate in England. His slaves built well: the old cream-colored mansion remains standing, a familiar landmark on the Virginia hills.

The fate of Arlington was sealed in 1831, when G.W.P. Custis's only daughter, Mary Anna Randolph Custis, married a promising young Army lieutenant named Robert E. Lee in the mansion's white parlor. They settled in and raised seven children there, a place, Lee wrote, where his "attachments are more strongly placed than at any other place in the world."[31]

Upon her father's death in 1857, Mary Custis Lee inherited the property, which included 196 slaves. Her husband set them to work improving the plantation and repairing the house, but his family's tenure at Arlington was cut short in 1861, when the Civil War broke out. Lee resigned his commission, cast his fortunes with Virginia, and turned against old Army friends and comrades he had known since his days as a West Point cadet. Union forces seized the strategically placed plantation and its mansion, established camps along the river, and built Freedman's Village as a refuge for more than a thousand former slaves. As war deaths mounted and existing graveyards in the capital filled with burials, authorities established a new national cemetery at Arlington in 1864. By the end of the war, more than ten thousand graves encircled the mansion and riddled the surrounding hills, making the place uninhabitable. The Lees never returned to live there.[32]

In the postwar years, federal officials rearranged some parts of the plantation and carved up the rest. They expanded the cemetery from two hundred acres to four hundred, established a premier cavalry outpost, later known as Fort Myer, on two hundred and fifty acres, and transformed about four hundred acres of bottomland into the Government Experimental Farm. Established in 1900, this sprawling farm occupied land that was then outside the cemetery walls, lying between Arlington Ridge Road and the river. Managed by the Department of

Agriculture, the farm was laid out in long test plots, green-houses, and laboratories, where scientists measured various strains of soybeans for the best oil content; developed new hyacinths, daffodils, and roses; established plots of hemp; introduced Brazilian tobacco resistant to black root rot; and conducted research on the expansibility of popcorn kernels.[33]

This pastoral chapter of Arlington's history faded as World War II approached, the nation mobilized, and the capital city spread to accommodate an influx of wartime workers. In 1940 the agricultural research station was moved to Beltsville, Maryland. On one corner of the old farm, the scattered offices of the War Department were consolidated into a massive new Pentagon, built to accommodate 24,000 work-ers. An adjoining two hundred acres of the research farm were set aside for South Post of Fort Myer, an expansion of the base devoted to new barracks, office space, and recreation halls. Where the graves of Section 60 lie today, the Federal Works Administration raised ten apartment buildings to house the single women converging on Washington for new jobs at the Pentagon and other federal offices. This housing complex, called Arlington Farms, had room for seven thou-sand residents.[34] They lived in two-story structures, named for states, and built with fiberboard walls known as "cemesto," a composite of sugarcane filaments, asbestos, and cement popular in wartime construction. The complex, officially dedicated by First Lady Eleanor Roosevelt in 1943,[35] had the dreary gray look of temporary barracks but won praise from the *Washington Post*'s art critic, impressed by "how much thoughtful architectural designing and planning, judicious use of color, and the introduction of cheerful fabrics in the interior furnishings have done to lighten the barracks-like effect of the dormitories." Like other housing projects in the neighborhood—and the armed forces at large—Arlington Farms was segregated.[36]

The new residents, affectionately termed "G-Girls" in news stories of the day, were assigned to jobs in the uniformed services and civilian bureaus as typists, file clerks, and secretaries who kept the war machinery humming. They also proved to be a magnet for thousands of lonely soldiers, sailors, and other service members who swarmed to regular open houses and dances at Arlington Farms. By 1945 the hospitality of the place was so widely established that when four American soldiers, recently escaped from Japanese prison camp, came to Washington for debriefings, the first place they asked to see was Arlington Farms, known by then as the "G-Girl Haven." One soldier reported that he had "found *the* girl" there.[37]

When the war ended, the G-Girls drifted away. Their dormitories emptied, and many of the buildings were bulldozed to make room for expanded operations at South Post of Fort Myer, which sprouted housing for married service members, barracks for WACs, an enlisted men's bar, and a movie theater. By 1950, when the latest conflict broke out on the Korean Peninsula, a draft center was brought into service by combining a couple of the old dormitories where G-Girls had so recently danced their nights away.[38]

South Post changed little until the death of President John F. Kennedy in November 1963. His nationally televised funeral, viewed by more than 41 million people, transformed the landscape at Arlington with the swiftness of an Old Testament cataclysm. Shocked citizens, watching as one as a president's funeral unfolded on grainy black-and-white screens, were powerfully moved by the spectacle, with its Black Watch pipers, howitzer salutes, and gathering of foreign dignitaries, all focused on the hillside below the old Lee mansion. The whole nation watched the president's young widow step from the crowd to light the eternal flame—a glimmer of light at one of the country's darkest moments.[39]

The memory of that weekend remained with all who witnessed it. An unexpected flood of visitors washed over Arlington, where they wished to see in reality what they had seen on television weeks before. Seven million visitors converged on Arlington in 1964, more than triple the number from previous years. The national cemetery was poorly prepared for this influx, which clogged streets and sidewalks, killed the grass, and led to a ban on cars throughout the cemetery. The crowding also prompted a $2.5 million redesign and reconstruction for JFK's tomb, which was improved with new landscaping, broader walkways, and permanent plantings still in service today.[40]

Kennedy's funeral also inspired many veterans, who decided that if Arlington was good enough for JFK, it was good enough for them too. In the years following Kennedy's death, the number of burials at Arlington jumped from four thousand to seven thousand a year. This fresh demand for graves, along with the demographic pressure from aging veterans of the Greatest Generation, caused planners at the Department of Defense to tighten burial qualifications at Arlington. At the same time they expanded the cemetery by a third of its former size. This extension, which added more than two hundred acres from South Post of Fort Myer and brought the cemetery to its present size of 624 acres, also included plans for a columbarium, where the cremated remains of service members and their families could be stored in the walls of a courtyard. With a capacity for fifty thousand inurnments, this development did much to conserve future space at Arlington.[41]

The new additions to the cemetery, bounded by Arlington Ridge Road on one side and by riverine acreage on the other, covered the land that had been worked by Lee family slaves, tilled by the Agriculture Department, settled by G-Girls, and occupied by soldiers from Fort Myer in earlier times. Now it took on a new, austere appearance, comprised of broad green meadows and ranks of simple white tombstones stretching to every horizon. Parceled into fifteen sections and crisscrossed with roads, the new cemetery grounds were brought into service in the mid-1970s. Arlington Ridge Road, historically the cemetery's eastern boundary from Civil War days, was renamed Eisenhower Drive; it is now Arlington's major north-south thoroughfare, providing access to the cemetery's most active area, including Section 60. Set on an east-west axis, Section 60 lies in a corridor connecting the Tomb of the Unknowns on the heights with the columbarium just east of Marshall Drive, and beyond that, to the monumental core of the capital city across the river.

Decades before Russell Rippetoe and his contemporaries came back from Iraq and Afghanistan, Section 60 received thousands of veterans who had fought in World War II, Korea, and Vietnam, lived to old age, and earned a place at Arlington. They occupy more than half of the space in Section 60. Their new neighbors, young men and women cut down in their prime, have been steadily filling the rows since Rippetoe's arrival in 2003, and in the process, they have changed the look and feel of the cemetery.

"It's not like any other part of Arlington," said Ami Neiberger-Miller, whose brother, Army Spec. Christopher T. Neiberger, was killed in Iraq in 2007. He lies in Grave No. 60-8650, a few paces from the sheltering trees of York Drive. "Section 60 is alive, more active. It's the one place we can come to make a connection with our brothers, husbands, and families. This is our memorial for Iraq and Afghanistan, like the Vietnam Wall was for their generation."[42]

Like the Vietnam Wall, Section 60 inspires friends and family to bring all manner of gifts to those buried there, making it more heavily decorated than older parts of the cemetery. The flowers come in every imaginable species and in every conceivable configuration, from red-white-and-blue bouquets, to single day lilies, to sprays of yellow roses, to wreaths of green carnations festooned with cans of Guinness— this last for Marine Sgt. Sean T. Callahan. A woman named Carol Ward Thomas, whose late husband was a Navy captain and is buried across Bradley Drive in Section 66, arrives in Section 60 after church each Sunday with a handful of flow- ers—usually red carnations or roses—which she distributes for her "boys," as she calls them, the sailors claimed by fighting in Iraq and Afghanistan. She is on a first-name basis with many of them, as well as their families. Runners from nearby florist shops also work the territory, buzzing up and down the aisles making deliveries between the tombstones, often for families who live too far away to visit but not so far that they have forgotten. All the florists need is a name, a grave number, and the 22211 zip code.[43]

Others bring personal offerings, with which they pay trib- ute and sometimes, perhaps, ease a dead warrior's passage to another world, just as the ancient Chinese and Egyptians did for those they loved. Someone leaves a new can of Copenhagen snuff for Staff Sgt. Adam L. Dickmyer; a stuffed rabbit with a basketball for Master Sgt. Tulsa Tulaga Tuliau; a Valentine card for Staff Sgt. Joshua Micah Mills; a rock with a Merry Christmas message for Sgt. Christopher M. Wilson; a cigar and a rubber duck in combat cammies for Staff Sgt. Jimmy Malachowski; a pair of "Happy Birthday" balloons for Cpl. Carlos J. Melendez; a pirate flag and chil- dren's pictures for Senior Chief Petty Officer Thomas J. Valentine; a yellow token from Spanky's Bar for Sgt. Christopher Hrbek; wild turkey feathers for a long line of Navy SEALS; a plastic dashboard monkey in a grass skirt for Sgt. First Class Christopher D. Henderson; a pack of Slim Jims and a brace of Bud Lights for Sgt. James R. McIlvaine; a fluorescent yellow Safety Patrol belt for Spec. Kelly Joseph

Mixon; a kiss, rendered in red lipstick on white stone, for Spec. Daniel Adrian Suplee; and the following message, scrawled on a rock with a green Sharpie, for Staff Sgt. Anthony N. Warigi: "Dear Dad, It's me Isabella. I am 10 years old. I never got to tell you that you are the favorite thing in my life . . . and I love you."[44]

Many visitors come to Section 60 bearing gifts of alcohol, a farewell ritual as old as the Trojan Wars, when Achilles mourned his dead friend Patroclus by pouring wine onto the ground "until it drenched the earth."[45] Despite a ban on alcohol at Arlington, the Homeric tradition thrives in Section 60. Friends and comrades kneel by graves to share drinks with a buddy, one sip for the living, one in the ground for the dead, and so on until the bottle or can runs dry. At times the good earth of Arlington fairly squelches underfoot. Authorities usually look the other way, but on occasion an officious person will drive up, emerge from his patrol car, and remind grieving visitors of the prohibition.

"So this cop walks up, tells me there's no drinking allowed, and says he'll have to take the bottle," said Mary Coyer, a buoyant, no-nonsense mother who had driven all the way from Michigan to have a beer with her dead son Ryan, an Army Ranger who finished six deployments before his arrival at Arlington on May 2, 2012.[46]

"Really?" she said, fixing the young officer with a stare and pouring half of the beer onto her son's grave, then half into herself before passing the empty bottle to the cop. "No way was that guy getting Ryan's beer!"[47]

It falls to Roderick Gainer, a professional historian and curator from the Army's Center of Military History, to sort through the thousands of items that turn up in Section 60 to determine which ones should be preserved, thrown away, or left in place. Some visitors carefully laminate pictures or letters in plastic before leaving them at graves; others weight items with rocks or skewer them in the grass with knitting needles; many leave things to be carried off by the wind or melted by the rain, with no expectation that their offerings will last. Gainer collects items of historical interest but must avoid contaminating the Army's vast collection of battle flags, uniforms, and other significant artifacts stored in a climate-controlled warehouse at nearby Fort Belvoir.

"Anything organic, like a candy bar or a bunch of flowers, we leave in place," said Gainer. "If a photograph or a letter has been sitting out in the rain, there's the danger that it will pick up mold or mildew. So we leave it. We've got stuff all the way back to the Revolutionary War in our collection and can't risk compromising it." Cemetery workers collect and dispose of flowers and other perishable items on weekly sweeps through the cemetery. Gainer, usually assisted by another historian, comes through every couple of weeks, searching for the artifacts that say something about the recent wars and the people who fought them.[48]

On a recent sweep, he spent a couple of hours picking his way among the tombstones, collecting empty rifle cartridges, photographs, military challenge coins, uniform patches, medals, and letters. He photographed the graves where artifacts were found and bagged each item in its own plastic bag. Each find is recorded in a database, which contains thousands of items from Section 60.

"You'd be surprised what we find," said Gainer, an excitable, fast-talking man who offered a few examples: "A sonogram of an unborn child. A Minié ball from the Civil War. A toy bird that dances when you squeeze its wing. Keys from a hotel in Kuwait. Tickets for an Alabama football game. Lots of tickets like that. Baseball caps. Baseballs.[49] All the things a young guy might have enjoyed."[50]

Over years of scouring Section 60, Gainer has noticed

patterns. "You see who gets visitors and who doesn't," he said. "Some graves are loaded with stuff. Some never get anything." A few paces from the curb at York Drive, he noted a concentration of graves from 2007—the time when thousands of reservists were pressed into duty to shore up operations in Iraq. Nearby a line of new graves from August 6, 2011, stood for the deadliest day for American forces in Afghanistan: a Chinook helicopter, on its way to a firefight in Wardak Province, was brought down by a Taliban grenade, killing all thirty members of a special operations squad, including Navy SEALs, Army pilots and crew, and three airmen. Seventeen of those killed lie side by side today in Section 60, where it is hard to walk in any direction without coming upon other graves belonging to members of the special ops fraternity—SEALs, Rangers, Green Berets, pararescue airmen, and chopper pilots, all of whom have carried much of the burden in the recent wars. "Those are the guys going out all the time," said Gainer.[51]

One also noticed that a number of new arrivals in Section 60 have helped diversify the neighborhood. Banned from combat assignments in Iraq or Afghanistan, many women have nonetheless been drawn closer to the fighting—as pilots, truck drivers, logisticians, and supply officers—which has increased their presence in Arlington. "It tells you something new about this war," said Gainer. "Every one is different. Every one has its own character, and you see that played out here."[52]

As Gainer talked and cataloged objects, he dragged a rolling plastic crate behind him, gradually filling the box with artifacts—a sealed letter from one grave: a blue Ranger tab, or shoulder patch, from another; a challenge coin from the Army's Tenth Mountain Division; two euro notes; one dollar bill; a quarter; a plastic dog; a jar of sand.

A jar of sand?

"Maybe from this guy's favorite beach?" Gainer speculated, returning the jar to its place on the grass before picking up a photograph a few rows over. The image, printed in sepia tones, depicted seven Navy SEALs dressed as cowboys, posing in borrowed hats, bandannas, and long duster coats, with a Wild West saloon scene as a backdrop.

"Who's the girl?" someone asked, pointing to a pretty woman seated among the cowboys.

"We don't know," said Gainer, studying the picture, "maybe a wife or girlfriend. But we know each of the guys. We have their names. They all went down in the Chinook." He returned the picture, propping it against a SEAL's headstone. "We've got that one and we don't need duplicates." If photographs are in good condition and not glued or taped to the tombstones, Gainer usually takes them for the archives. "We want to have a face associated with every tombstone—that's the goal," he said. "A lot of the men who died in World War I, we don't know what they looked like. We didn't have pictures. That

A friend leaves a picture of Navy SEALs, dressed up as cowboys, at their graves in Section 60. (Robert M. Poole)

will not happen again. Everyone here will have something in the archives." Gainer swept his hand over the tombstones, then resumed his survey, dragging his rolling crate through the thick grass.[53]

"Whoa, look at this," he said, stopping to study a photograph of a young soldier partying with friends, laughing it up. "So young!" he sighed. "Just kids."

"Even after three years on this project, it still gets to me." He moved down the line, squinting away a tear.[54]

3

ABOVE AND BEYOND

NAVIGATING AMONG THE tombstones of Section 60 on a December afternoon, Judy Meikle found the one she was looking for a few strides north of Bradley Drive. She placed a heart-shaped rock before Grave No. 60-9088 and settled in to pass the time with Cpl. Benjamin S. Kopp, a twenty-one-year-old Army Ranger who died in 2009 as a result of combat injuries from Afghanistan.

At sixty-one, with smartly coiffed gray hair and a straight-backed bearing, Meikle could have easily passed for one of the Gold Star mothers who patrol this corner of Arlington daily, talking to the dead and tidying their graves.* But she had never met Kopp. She had no family. And she was unrelated to the Ranger she had traveled halfway across the continent to visit. Meikle was

---

* The Gold Star Mothers of America, founded in 1928 for those who had lost sons in World War I, now represents all families with loved ones killed in wartime. Following a tradition begun in the last century, Gold Star families often hang a star in their windows as a symbol of their sacrifice.

able to make the journey only because the dead man's heart had been thumping away in her chest since the summer of 2009, giving life to a woman who almost certainly would have died without it.

"I'm the recipient of a miracle," she said in an interview from her home in Winnetka, Illinois. For months, until Ben Kopp's misfortune provided deliverance, she had been in steady decline from a congenital heart ailment and hoping that a suitable transplant would turn up. "I can tell you it's no fun waiting on the threshold of death," she said. "But four years later I'm doing great, thanks to Ben. I'm Army strong. There isn't a day that goes by that I don't think of him and thank him."[1]

Nothing can bring back a young life lost to war, but if the intertwined tale of Ben Kopp and Judy Meikle is any sign, some good can be salvaged from the worst possible tragedy, even one brewed in the dust and smoke of Afghanistan's most violent state, Helmand Province, which has claimed the lives of more coalition service members than any other in that tortured land.[2]

Ben Kopp arrived in Afghanistan three years after finishing

Cpl. Benjamin S. Kopp downrange. (Stephenson family photo)

Jill Stephenson and her son Ben Kopp, between deployments.
(Stephenson family photo)

high school in Rosemount, Minnesota, where he struggled to earn his diploma in 2006. He left home for the Army a few weeks later, thrived in the structure and physicality of the service, and earned the coveted black and gold shoulder tab of an Army Ranger at Fort Benning, Georgia. His on-the-job training as a rifleman included two combat tours in Iraq with the Third Battalion of the 75th Ranger Regiment before he landed, in May 2009, in Afghanistan.

There, in a fateful firefight with Taliban insurgents, he took a bullet to the knee on July 10, 2009. The shot severed Kopp's popliteal artery and caused profuse bleeding, which surgeons in a battalion hospital were trying to repair when Kopp suffered a heart attack from the massive loss of blood. The doctors got his heart going again, but Kopp never regained consciousness. Transferred first to the Landstuhl Regional Medical Center in Germany, then to Walter Reed Army Medical Center in Washington, he was kept in an induced coma to reduce the damaging effects of cerebral hypoxia.

Kopp's mother, Jill Stephenson, flew in from Minnesota to join him at Walter Reed on July 14. She kept vigil at her son's bedside, assessing his prospects and updating a wide network of friends and family about the young soldier's condition.

"He is full of tubes and wires and cords and bags and bandages and tape and everything you can imagine the most critical person to look like," she wrote on the website CaringBridge that summer. "We have to wait and see what happens over the next day or two. We still need a miracle."[3]

Despite Kopp's fighting spirit, Stephenson's prayers, and the good wishes of thousands who followed his story from a distance, his health worsened. After a few days, his family began to consider removing him from life support. Doctors told Stephenson that "Ben's brain could not sustain itself to any level of normalcy," she reported, "and if he survived, his quality of life would be poor, at best. We came to terms with the reality of his fate and began talking about organ donation."[4]

Every young warrior leaves home feeling invincible. But anticipating the worst, the services require all men and women, before deployment, to fill out a sheaf of official forms known as the Blue Book designating next of kin, power of attorney, religious affiliation, and other particulars, including funeral plans down to the place of burial, the names of honorary pallbearers, and the hymns to be played. The Blue Book also has space, in section 2, line 25, for soldiers to donate their organs; Kopp had checked the "yes" box in that category before his last flight to Afghanistan.[5]

"Ben had no hesitation about that, none at all," Stephenson said. "We had always talked about organ donation in our family and we were comfortable with it. That is because of something that happened to my own brother, J.T., when he was eleven. He was hit by a car and killed, and we made the decision to donate his organs. That was 1982." Although Kopp was not born until six years later, he grew up hearing about his uncle J.T.'s untimely death and his parting gift, which gave life to others. "Ben knew our family were pioneers in this area long before others were willing to donate organs," she said. "We were proud of that."[6]

Eight days after her son's combat injury, Stephenson made the difficult decision to allow surgeons to remove his heart, liver, kidneys, and other organs. She notified friends of her intentions on the CaringBridge website, which caught the eye of Maria Burund, a Kopp family relative who had worked with Judy Meikle in Chicago. Burund had been tracking Meikle's travails on a separate website called "Judy's Ticker," established by friends in the Chicago area. Burund wondered if the dying soldier's heart might provide a match for Meikle. Burund called Stephenson, who readily agreed to designate Meikle as the recipient for her son's heart. Because Stephenson wanted to keep Ben's name alive, she also signed waivers allowing Meikle and others to know their benefactor's identity.[7]

"That was just the first hurdle," said Meikle, who had been on the waiting list for a heart for seventy-seven days and on antirejection drugs for seven months. "But you still have to determine if there is a three-way match for the transplant. You need the same blood type. You need a tissue match. And the heart has to fit—it can't be too big or too small. Well, we hit those markers one after another. All the stars lined up, and I knew before I got Ben's heart where it came from."[8]

He was removed from the respirator and died on July 18. His organs were dispatched to waiting recipients, including Meikle, who received his heart at Northwestern Memorial Hospital in Chicago on July 20. Just nine days after that, Meikle was sent home to recover. Friends took away the keys to her Audi convertible to discourage unsupervised outings. She was still convalescing at home on August 7 when Ben Kopp was laid to rest at Arlington.[9]

It was a steamy day with a high temperature of eighty-six

"We're old friends now," says Judy Meikle, who makes regular visits to Ben Kopp's grave. (Meikle family photo)

degrees and the cloying humidity that threatened to wilt the sharp blue uniforms of the Old Guard's firing party and the crisp green perfection of the Rangers, up from Georgia to pay homage to one of their own. The flags were folded and passed, one for Stephenson and one for her former husband, Duane Kopp, who sat with her on the front row. They were surrounded by friends. A procession of dignitaries passed down the line, offering handshakes, words of comfort, and the occasional hug: Robert Gates, secretary of defense; Pete Geren, secretary of the army; and Minnesota's newest senator, Al Franken, all came to express sympathy and show support.[10]

Meikle could not make the journey on her own, so five of her friends did it for her, joining the throng in Section 60 that day. When the service was finished, all five Chicagoans piled into one car and raised Meikle on the speakerphone to relay a play-by-play of Kopp's final honors. "We all cried together," Meikle recalled. "Then they went to a reception with Ben's Ranger friends who had been all dressed up for the funeral. Now they were in their shorts and T-shirts having beers and telling stories about Ben. My friends called and filled me in on that too—the next best thing to being there."[11]

Kopp's mother never regretted Ben's burial at Arlington. "It's what he wanted and he's where he should be, surrounded by heroes of every generation," she said. "It's a longer drive for me, but I like being there. I can see from the things his friends leave that he's getting lots of traffic. He's not forgotten. There's so much comfort in that."[12]

As new turf took root over Kopp's grave, parts of him went to work not only in Judy Meikle but also in others. "One man in the Washington area got Ben's liver," said Jill Stephenson. "I heard he's doing well—going on four years now. Another man got a kidney—he's still alive. Fred Thurston got Ben's other kidney, which kept him alive for eight months. He didn't make it, unfortunately. He died from other causes, but I've heard from his son and wife, who told me they were very grateful that they had those extra months with him. These donations have a ripple effect, you know. So many people are inspired by these stories, they become organ donors. And Ben keeps living on and on."[13]

Where does one life end and another begin? The boundaries sometimes blur. It may be just a coincidence, but in the years since her transplant, Judy Meikle has developed an inexplicable craving for green beans, which she had detested for half a century. When she told Jill Stephenson about it, there was stunned silence on the telephone line.[14]

"Oh . . . my . . . gosh!" said Stephenson. "That was Ben's favorite dish. That's what he always ordered when we went to Ruth's Chris Steak House. He wasn't as interested in the steak, just the beans."[15]

Four years on and showing no signs of rejection, Meikle has been able to cut back on postoperative medication. "Ben and I have learned to coexist," she said. She has also become a tireless proselytizer for transplants, speaking at Rotary Clubs, intensive care units, and other venues on a monthly basis. "An average of eighteen people die every day waiting for organs." She shifted into her sales mode. "You don't need to be an Army Ranger to be a hero. Register to donate like Ben did." The former mortgage broker is a formidable advocate, fearless about putting the squeeze on complete strangers after one of her speeches. "I ask them to show me their driver's license to see if they're a donor," she said. "If they're not, I have the paperwork so they can sign up on the spot, which you can do in Illinois."[16]

A new friendship has flourished between Meikle and Stephenson, who receives a Mother's Day card and flowers from Meikle each year. "She's the mother of my heart," said Meikle. "If she hadn't had Ben, I wouldn't be here, so I express my gratitude." Stephenson's family has also adopted Meikle as one of their own. "I don't have a family, but Ben has provided one for me—all his people call me Aunt Judy now."[17]

When Meikle and Stephenson meet, Ben's mother always goes through the same greeting ceremony, asking to feel her son's heart. The ritual was recorded by a Minnesota television station for Thanksgiving a few years ago.

"It always beats faster when I touch it," said Stephenson, pressing a hand to Meikle's chest.

"It does," said Meikle. "It knows you."

"I know," said Stephenson. She smiled. So did Meikle.[18]

In an age often known for its greed and selfishness, Ben Kopp's farewell gift would seem to be an exception. It is not. The evidence lies all around him at Arlington, in the graves of men and women who sacrificed themselves for comrades without a moment's hesitation. This urge runs counter to the most basic survival instinct, but it has been a central tenet of the soldier's creed since the time of Thermopylae, when the Spartans stood, fought, and died together in 480 B.C.[19] In all the years since, combatants have explored why one soldier would be willing to give up his life for another, none more eloquently than historian William Manchester, who fought in the most brutal Pacific battles of World War II before being severely wounded on Okinawa. "Those men on the line were my family," the Marine wrote. "They were closer to me than I can say, closer than any friends had ever been or ever would be. They had never let me down, and I couldn't do it to them . . . Men, I now knew, do not fight for flag or country, for the Marine Corps or glory or any other abstraction. They fight for one another." Like every good warrior before him, Manchester would risk death before failing his brothers-in-arms.[20]

That brotherly instinct brought Army Pfc. Ross A. McGinnis to Section 60 at age nineteen. He saved four soldiers in the Iraq War on December 4, 2006, when an insurgent on a rooftop tossed a grenade into the turret of his Humvee in the Adhamiyah neighborhood of northeastern Baghdad. McGinnis, the turret gunner, saw the grenade, tried to bat it away, and watched it tumble past him into the vehicle.

"Grenade!" he shouted. "It's in the truck!"[21]

Instead of jumping out of the hatch and running to safety as his training dictated, McGinnis dropped into the Humvee and pounced on the grenade, pinning it to the radio bank with his back to shield Sgt. Lyle Buehler, Sgt. First Class Cedric Thomas, Spec. Sean Lawson, and Staff Sgt. Ian Newland from the blast. McGinnis, a sinewy six-footer weighing 136 pounds, absorbed the force of the explosion and died on the spot. His comrades survived. All but Newland, wounded by shrapnel and the blast force, returned to duty. McGinnis was posthumously promoted to specialist and received the Medal of Honor, the nation's highest military decoration, for his "conspicuous gallantry and intrepidity at the risk of his life above and beyond the call of duty."[22]

"The driver and truck commander I am certain would have

A gold seal marks the gravestone of Spec. Ross A. McGinnis and other
Medal of Honor recipients at Arlington. (Robert M. Poole)

been killed if that blast had taken full effect," said Maj. Michael Baka, who at the time was commander of McGinnis's company in the First Battalion, 26th Infantry Regiment. "He's supposed to announce the grenade, give a fair amount of time for people in the vehicle to react, and then he's supposed to save himself. No one would have blamed him if he did that, because that is what he was trained to do."[23]

Newland, who still bears the scars from that day, was diagnosed with traumatic brain injury and post-traumatic stress disorder and medically retired from the Army. He has no doubt about why McGinnis jumped between him and the grenade. "Why he did it? Because we were his brothers. He loved us," said Newland.[24] "He gave me a life that he can't have now. There isn't a single day . . . that goes by that I don't take in everything—the smell of my daughter's hair, the smile my son gives me out of nowhere, the soft touch of my wife's hand . . . things people might take for granted. I'm able to . . . have these things . . . every day, every hour, because of what Ross did."[25]

Like more than three hundred other Medal of Honor

recipients at Arlington, McGinnis has a distinctive tombstone, with the medal's five-pointed star and profile of the Roman goddess Minerva painted in gold under his name. As the only Medal of Honor laureate from Iraq or Afghanistan at Arlington, he gets frequent visitors, especially school groups from his native Pennsylvania. Arriving on buses, they constitute a boisterous, high-energy mob when they sweep down York Drive and storm into Section 60, but they usually go very quiet when a teacher leads them to McGinnis's grave and explains how he got there. They often leave flowers, notes, and other tokens of esteem at Grave No. 60-8544, where Ross McGinnis lies. He went off to war as a teenager—about their age.

McGinnis, never known as an outstanding student growing up in Knox, Pennsylvania, was hyperactive, always on the go. He could not sit still, said his father, Tom McGinnis, who works in a NAPA Auto Parts store. Although proud of the recognition his son has received, the elder McGinnis bristled at the suggestion that Ross should be considered more than ordinary. "He'd remind you more of Bart Simpson than anything else," he told a local reporter. "You know, sort of an underachiever." He told another interviewer: "He wasn't exceptional. He was just like you and me. He just made a split-second decision. He did what he thought was right. That doesn't make him extraordinary. He just did an extraordinary thing."[26]

Heroes are ordinary people who do extraordinary things. One dodges fire to pull a wounded soldier to safety; another parachutes behind enemy lines to rescue stranded comrades; another walks point through fields seeded with improvised explosive devices—all deeds you hear about if you hang around Section 60 a few days.

Few people who knew Andrew Joseph Baddick in his hometown of Jim Thorpe, Pennsylvania, would have considered him a hero, unless you counted his heroic capacity for Bud Lights or his fearlessness on the Lehigh River, where he worked as a whitewater guide before joining the Army in 1999. His own mother, Ann Adams, said the boy, known to everyone as "A.J.," was a handful. "He was just a kid with a lot of mischief in him. I wouldn't let him have an iguana, so he sneaked off and got one tattooed on his shoulder. That's the kind of kid he was. If you told him not to dive off the bridge, that's the next thing he'd do." After she divorced Joseph M. Baddick, A.J.'s father, Ann became partners with Jack Adams, who helped raise A.J., taught him to swim, and showed him how to handle a boat. "From the time he was eight A.J. loved the water," said his mother. "He practiced rolling his kayak in the river behind the train station over and over again. He was generous—the kind of guy who would give his last dime to somebody on the street."[27]

Although Baddick rarely saw his father, he looked up to the former paratrooper, vowing to join the Army's 82nd Airborne Division and wear the maroon beret, just as his old man had done. A.J. sailed through basic training at Fort Hood, Texas, and headed for the rigors of jump school at Fort Benning, Georgia, so confident of the outcome that he had an airborne tattoo inked on his arm before starting the course. When he finished, he was assigned to the 82nd Airborne at Fort Bragg, North Carolina, in 2001.[28]

"When he came home from training, we went grocery shopping together and I couldn't reach something on the top shelf," Ann Adams recalled. "He said, 'Here, let me get that for you.' And I'm wondering, *Who is this kid they've sent back to me?* Looked like A.J., but it wasn't him. He cut back on the beer. He took responsibility. The Army made him into a real man."[29]

Resolved to make the military his career, Baddick reenlisted after his first tour, rising to the rank of sergeant and serving in Afghanistan. Between training and deployments, he took time to marry Jami Sydensticker in Pennsylvania. The marriage fell apart in less than a year, in part because of Baddick's frequent absences. "He liked being in the military for the most part," said Sydensticker, who now lives near Pittsburgh, "but it is definitely not a place to have a relationship." Baddick was single again when he arrived in Iraq in the summer of 2003, a few weeks after President George W. Bush announced in May, under the "Mission Accomplished" banner, that combat operations had ended in that country.[30]

In reality, the fighting was just heating up. Baddick and other troops were soon embroiled with local insurgents, who harassed U.S. forces with small-arms fire, suicide bombs, and mortar attacks as the year unfolded. Baddick and comrades from the First Battalion of the 504th Paratroop Infantry Regiment were drawn into danger on the outskirts of Baghdad, where enemy forces rained mortars on Abū Gharaib Prison, at that time an unknown dot on the map before the place-name became synonymous with abuse and torture of inmates.

Members of Baddick's battalion, joining forces with troops from the 223rd Military Police Company of the Kentucky National Guard, piled into five Humvees and roared away from the prison on September 29 with the intention of ambushing enemy mortar positions near Abū Gharaib. It was after nine P.M., with dusk settling over the capital. The lead vehicle, loaded with Kentucky Guardsmen, swerved off the road near a deep irrigation canal. The Humvee spun out in a muddy field, causing the following vehicle, also occupied by Kentuckians, to veer around the stalled truck, overshoot the road, and plunge into the canal, rolling over on its side in twelve feet of water. Four soldiers in the truck, weighed down with body armor and other equipment, scrambled out of the wreck and were swept downstream in the strong current. Two were floundering toward shore and being helped onto land when Baddick's Humvee, the third of the convoy, rumbled onto the scene.[31]

The last known photograph of Sgt. A. J. Baddick, recipient of the Soldier's Medal for heroism in Iraq. (Adams family photo)

He jumped out and raced toward the wreck, stripping off his body armor and helmet on the run, and dove into the murky, swirling water to pull Spec. Rodney Pence to safety on the bank, not far from where Sgt. First Class David R. Jaeckel stood at the water's edge. Jaeckel had his eye on the spot where the fourth man from the truck, Sgt. Darrin Potter, had disappeared. "I reached for his hands, but I only could grab his fingers and he slipped out of my grasp," Jaeckel said of Potter. "The current and the weight of his body armor pulled him under the bridge."[32]

Jaeckel shouted to Baddick, still in the water, and pointed to where Potter had gone under.[33]

"I got him," said Baddick, diving into the current and disappearing in the gloom. It was the last thing he said. He was twenty-six.[34]

His comrades, aided by Air Force pararescue specialists and Special Forces divers, spent the next eighteen hours scouring the canal for his body, finally retrieving him and Potter, the Guardsman he had tried to save. Both had been battered, tangled in underwater debris, and pinned down by the strong current.[35] Friends and family who knew Baddick as a powerful swimmer thought that he might have hit his head on the submerged truck and been knocked unconscious before he drowned.[36]

If the particulars of Baddick's death were inconclusive, there was no doubt about the motive that had propelled him into the water. Maj. John J. Marr, investigating the accident for the Army, concluded that Baddick "acted heroically, instinctively, and alone to try and save the life of a fellow soldier . . . Sgt. Baddick was neither ordered nor instructed to attempt this rescue. The speed of the canal's current could not reasonably be detected given the time of day and light conditions. The immediacy of the situation precluded any notions of attempting to tie a safety-line or rope to Sgt. Baddick . . . Given Sgt. Baddick's experience as a river guide and sense of duty . . . he likely felt the most qualified and competent person to attempt to rescue Sgt. Potter and would probably have acted in the same manner regardless."[37]

It was 9:20 the next night, September 30, when two soldiers in uniform appeared on Ann Adams's doorstep in Jim Thorpe.[38]

"Oh my God," she said, opening the door to the visitors. "What did he do? Has he been hurt?"[39]

"On behalf of the United States Army . . ." one of the men began, at which point Adams broke down, blocking out the rest of the casualty report but knowing, against all hope, that the worst had happened.[40] Her son came home a few days later, greeted by hundreds of neighbors who crowded Griffiths Funeral Home for an old-fashioned send-off. "I never seen so many people at a wake before or since," said one of the neighbors who turned out for the event.[41] The casket remained closed because Baddick had been badly disfigured from his time underwater.

The first hints of autumn color brushed the Pocono Mountains above Jim Thorpe the next day, October 10, when, after a funeral mass at St. Joseph's Catholic Church, a bagpiper led Baddick's casket and a huge crowd of neighbors through the narrow streets of town, just uphill from the river where the kid with the iguana tattoo had perfected his whitewater technique. Alerted by the screech of approaching pipers, a few regulars left their drinks at Gerber's Café on North Street, emerged into the sunlight, and formed a ragged line on the sidewalk, saluting one of their own, home from the wars and bound for final honors at Arlington.[42]

A decade has passed since Baddick arrived in Section 60, bringing him plenty of company from others killed in Iraq and Afghanistan. The years have done little to ease the loss Ann Adams still feels. "A.J. is in good company here," she said, gazing out at the ranks of white tombstones. "I am proud of him, but I'm still struggling with the fact that he's gone." She straightened his miniature Army Airborne flag and set out fresh roses for another Memorial Day at Arlington. "I had to close his bank account. I got the first things they sent back from Iraq, things he had on him, a Blessed Mother card, his wallet, his watch—this great big Army watch I wore for the longest time. I've been so preoccupied with A.J. that I was fired from my job and my family doesn't want to hear me talk about him anymore."[43]

Like others whose loved ones have died violently in combat, she clung to the hope that Baddick did not suffer. "I cannot stand the idea that he drowned," she said. "He was such a strong swimmer. They said that he may have hit his head on something and that knocked him out. I hope that's true. I have the autopsy report, but I don't want to read it." She handed it over, with a sheaf of other official papers.[44]

The report, issued after Baddick's postmortem examination at Dover Air Force Base in Delaware, was suggestive but hardly conclusive on the events that led to his drowning. He had no concussion, but his head had been cut in several places before he died—"antemortem contusions," in the medical examiner's language. He also wrote that there "was evidence . . . of minor head trauma that may have contributed to the drowning." He ruled the death an accident.[45]

Adams finds some comfort in the outpouring of sympathy from her son's friends and comrades, who have flooded the Fallen Heroes website and others like it with praise for Baddick. "Sgt. Baddick was an outstanding paratrooper," wrote a sergeant major who served with him in the 82nd Airborne Division. "He was especially proud to serve in the same unit that his father had served in. Andrew always carried a picture of his father with him and was quick to show it off . . . We were saddened but not surprised at the circumstances."[46] A soldier whose friend Darrin Potter had drowned with Baddick thanked him for making the effort: "I was out on patrol that night that this hero tried to save my friend. I personally never got the honor of meeting Andrew but know that one day we will meet and I will thank him."[47] Baddick's company commander, Capt. Richard R. Balestri, told Ann Adams that he had never seen such bravery in a soldier. Balestri and other comrades recommended Baddick not only for the Bronze Star Medal for meritorious service but also for the rarely awarded Soldier's Medal, given for heroism outside of combat. It is the noncombatant's equivalent of the Distinguished Service Cross. Baddick's posthumous awards were quickly approved and noted on a new tombstone at Arlington.[48]

"Even though A.J. was on combat patrol when he died, it's considered an accident," said Adams, sitting by her son's grave with his eight-year-old namesake and niece, Andi, daughter of Adams's daughter Elizabeth. They were waiting for President Obama, who often showed up for special occasions in Section 60, trailed by platoons of photographers and proceeded by a security detail that looked into coolers, scrutinized cars, and passed metal-detecting wands up and down the arms, legs, and private parts of every human within the bounds of York,

Marshall, Bradley, and Eisenhower Drives. Even former Adm. Michael Mullen, the retired chairman of the Joint Chiefs of Staff, now a civilian in a polo shirt and a floppy hat, dutifully raised his arms and took the wand, a fistful of red roses drooping in his right hand.

Up on the hill by the Tomb of the Unknowns, the Old Guard's saluting battery charged its howitzers and commenced a deep-throated twenty-one-gun salute for the president, who slid into a convoy and descended through the cemetery, heading for Section 60. A flutter of excitement, a leading edge of men in black, and the president and first lady came striding down the aisle of graves, exchanged hugs and handshakes with Ann Adams, walked over the grass where A.J.'s feet would be, and moved down the corridor of grieving families who surged forward to shake hands. Many of them, who often feel that the recent wars are forgotten, seemed to appreciate the president's gesture.[49]

Paula Davis, whose son Justin, killed in Afghanistan, lies a few steps from A.J. Baddick's grave, gave Obama credit for showing up. "This is the third or fourth time I've seen him here. We're old friends."[50]

"What did he say?" someone asked.

"He said, 'There's my girl,' and I got a big hug," she said, surrounded by a clutch of friends and family in folding chairs pulled close to her son's grave.[51]

Not everyone welcomed the president's presence at Arlington, which can be just as political as any other venue in a contentious capital, even on Memorial Day. A pair of off-duty Marines, astride their motorcycles on Bradley Drive, pointedly gunned their engines and tendered middle-finger salutes for the president. Tom Heinlein, a father from Michigan, whose soldier son was killed by an IED in Iraq in 2007, glowered after Obama. "I've got no use for him," he said. "This day should be for families. What he's doing here is just for the media."[52]

★ ★ ★

The action that brought Baddick to Section 60 was an exceptional act of bravery, but the accidental nature of his death was not at all unusual. In the history of American warfare, almost as many service members have died from illness and accident as from bullets and bombs. The first conflict in which more were killed by combat injuries was World War II, which claimed 291,557 in battle, 113,842 from accidents and other causes. In Vietnam, the level of fatalities from noncombat causes spiked to 47 percent—with 42,786 service members dying from accident and illness, 47,434 in battle.

More than 6,000 Americans have died in the last decade of conflict in Iraq, Afghanistan, associated theaters of war, and on the home front. At least 1,378, or 27 percent, have died from nonbattle causes, including drowning, car accidents, aircraft crashes, training disasters, and thrill-seeking behavior, all of which have added new graves to Section 60 in recent years, among them those belonging to Lance Cpl. William T. Wild IV, a Marine who survived two tours of Afghanistan to die with seven others in a mortar training accident in Nevada; Sgt. Roger W. Halford I, twenty-eight, a member of the Old Guard at Fort Myer, killed in a motorcycle accident near Washington, D.C.; Senior Chief Petty Officer Thomas J. Valentine, thirty-seven, a Navy SEAL killed when his parachute failed in a training exercise in Arizona; Marine Sgt. Christopher J. Jacobs, twenty-nine, killed when his amphibious assault vehicle flipped during maneuvers at Twentynine Palms, California; and Marine Maj. Jeremy J. Graczyk, thirty-three, who, after several deployments to Afghanistan, died parachuting from the Eiger Mushroom in the Swiss Alps while on leave.*

---

* His parachute malfunctioned while he was BASE jumping—from Building, Antenna, Span, Earth. Aficionados of BASE jumping dive from buildings, towers, or other fixed sites and parachute to earth. Some enthusiasts, outfitted in wing suits, glide from the heights like flying squirrels.

One of the most bizarre accidents befell Marine Maj. Jeffrey C. Bland, thirty-seven, killed when a three-pound bird brought down the AH-1W Cobra helicopter he was piloting in September 2011. The bird, a female red-tailed hawk, flew into the top of the chopper, wrecked a critical link in the pitch-change mechanism, put the main rotor into violent vibration, caused it to separate from the aircraft, and sent the chopper plummeting to earth near Camp Pendleton, California, where the crash set off a brush fire that consumed more than 120 acres. Another pilot, on board when the training accident occurred, died with Bland.[53]

"The strangest thing is what happened after that," said Tristan Gale, a former roommate who was visiting her friend's grave in Section 60. "While they were going through the wreckage doing the investigation this hawk's mate kept circling the crash site, whistling for her." Gale, still dressed in sweats and running shoes from the 2012 Marine Marathon, had just completed the 10K portion of the race to honor the unlucky pilot. She gently patted his tombstone and headed for the exit, just hours before Tropical Storm Sandy raked through the cemetery, scattering flowers and soaking the grass.[54]

4

FROM WAR TO PEACE

A SIGNATURE INJURY OF the recent wars, post-traumatic stress disorder (PTSD) is an often debilitating condition, haunting hundreds of thousands of those who fought in Iraq and Afghanistan and consigning far too many of them to Arlington National Cemetery.

First recognized in 1980 in the American Psychiatric Association's *Diagnostic and Statistical Manual of Mental Disorders*, the malady is, in truth, nothing new: the illness, or something very much like it, has afflicted soldiers and sailors for as long as there has been warfare. Herodotus remarked upon a psychic trauma that knocked Greek warriors out of action as early as 490 B.C. That was when an Athenian soldier named Epizelus, facing a superior force of Persian enemies at the Battle of Marathon, went blind after the comrade next to him was struck dead by "a gigantic warrior with a huge beard." The psychological impact on Epizelus was instantaneous. He was "in the thick of the fray," Herodotus wrote, "behaving himself as a brave man should, when suddenly he was stricken with blindness, without blow of sword or dart; and this blindness continued thenceforth during the whole of his . . . life."[1] At the Battle of Thermopylae a decade later, Herodotus told of a Greek commander named Leonidas who held three hundred of his men out of battle because they were so psychologically wasted that they could no longer fight: they were "out of heart and unwilling to encounter the danger."[2]

In all the years since, every conflict has produced some variant of PTSD—the nightmares and social isolation that Shakespeare ascribed to Hotspur in *Henry IV, Part I*, the soldier's heart of the Civil War, the shell shock of World War I, the combat fatigue of World War II and Korea, the post-Vietnam Syndrome from that war. Even among combatants with no physical wounds, the trauma of a single event can trigger the clinical symptoms associated with PTSD—intrusive recollections, emotional numbing, and hyperarousal that incapacitate some veterans, who may suffer from panic, terror, dread, grief, despair, anger, and flashbacks, all of which make it difficult to resume civilian life when the bullets stop flying.[3]

Although most combatants weather the transition from battlefield to home front without being sidetracked by full-blown PTSD, more than 18 percent of those from the recent wars in Iraq and Afghanistan—some 296,000 of the 1.6 million deployed at the time of the most authoritative research by the Rand Corporation—are believed to suffer from PTSD or associated symptoms from traumatic brain injury (TBI). Another 900,000 men and women have gone to war since the Rand study was published in 2008, bringing the total of those deployed to 2.5 million. Thus the real universe of veterans affected by PTSD or TBI is likely to be as high as 462,000.[4] "As time goes on, those numbers will increase, just as they did in the years after Vietnam," said Bonnie Carroll, president and founder of the Tragedy Assistance Program for Survivors

(TAPS), a national support group for families of service members.[5]

Like others whose loved ones served in wartime, Liz Mocabee spent much of her married life worrying about her often absent husband, Master Sgt. Sean M. Mocabee, a decorated Green Beret assigned to the First Battalion of the Tenth Special Forces Group in Stuttgart, Germany. A medical sergeant equally skilled at healing and killing, Mocabee was on frequent deployment with his special operations unit, making forays into the hot zones of Iraq, Afghanistan, and Africa for most of the last decade. Even before the United States went to war in Iraq in 2003, Mocabee was there, training and equipping Kurdish fighters opposed to President Saddam Hussein in the 1990s.[6]

After the attacks of September 11, 2001, drew the United States into the current conflict, Mocabee was seldom far from the action, shuttling from his home base in Germany to Iraq to

Master Sgt. Sean Mocabee at Forward Operating Base Shank, Logar Province, Afghanistan. (Staff Sgt. Christian Mullins)

Afghanistan and back to Germany. "He was always on the go, either decompressing from deployment or getting his team ready for a new assignment," said Liz, herself an Army veteran who had met her future husband when both were studying Russian at the Defense Language Institute in Monterey, California. They married and had two children; she returned to civilian life, relocating to Germany with the family in 2006.[7]

Soldiers who worked and trained with Sean Mocabee knew him as a self-contained, level-headed professional, a steadying force in any high-danger situation. "He was the calm, quiet one in a crisis," said David V. Hill, a retired master sergeant who trained with Mocabee in the Army's rigorous school for special ops medics. "If you got in a situation where things got out of hand, Sean was the guy you'd want on your side. Somebody got in an argument, threw his hat down, started pointing fingers, and Sean was the one to calm things. And he'd be grinning," said Hill, a former Special Forces medic. "In those days the other guys would stay out partying all night, but Sean would have a few beers and go home to his family. He was always the serious, responsible guy."[8] Another of Mocabee's old comrades from their days in the 82nd Airborne, retired Master Sgt. Glenn G. Oliver, echoed Hill's comments. "Sean was the one out of all of us who had the most drive and took the whole military thing seriously," he said. "He was really driven—totally spun up."[9]

That drive and steadiness made Mocabee an exceptional soldier. But the wear and tear of repeated deployments began to show during his last mission to Afghanistan, which ran from October 2007 through April 2008. Over forty years old, contemplating retirement, and confronted with the daily prospect of violent death, Mocabee brooded about incidents he might have shrugged off on earlier assignments. He felt guilty for surviving an attack that killed a staff sergeant in his unit; he fumed about the sketchy intelligence reports that jeopardized his men; he resented the pettiness of officers who insisted on a spit-and-polish appearance for troops risking their lives in a hostile country; he could not shake the memory of a late-night raid, when he had almost stepped on an infant. "He saw this blanket moving across the floor, realized there was a baby inside, and kicked it away so that none of the guys behind him would crush it," said Liz. "That really got to him, and I could tell from his e-mails and the calls from Afghanistan that he was increasingly under severe stress." The tension slowly chipped away at Mocabee, who was determined to betray no sign of weakness or uncertainty—in the war zone or at home.[10]

Although none of his comrades in Afghanistan registered concerns about Mocabee's mental health, his wife, keeping in touch from afar, could feel his condition deteriorating. He became erratic, asking for a divorce in three separate e-mails, then apologizing and saying that he could not bear the thought of leaving his family. He had flashes of anger, fumed about command decisions, and sat alone in his quarters with his side-arm, contemplating suicide. He sent a chilling e-mail to Liz and the children that autumn: "In case I have not said it enough I will miss you all."[11]

As soon as she received that message, Liz asked chaplains in Afghanistan to check on her husband. They could not do so, they discovered, because Sean was on a mission, beyond reach, which kept Liz in suspense for another week. When he returned to his post and heard that his wife had been asking about him, he called home, told Liz that she had misconstrued his worrisome e-mail, and assured her that he was fine: he had no intention of harming himself, leaving his family, or abandoning his brothers-in-arms in the middle of a war. Liz repeated what she had said before: that she would wait for him in Germany "and that we could work through anything together."[12]

★   ★   ★

She hardly recognized the soldier who came home from Afghanistan that April. "The man who returned from that deployment was not my husband," she said.[13] "From the time he got home, he just got worse, spiraling down and down."[14] Still she loved him, and she knew that he loved her. He loved the children. But he could not make the transition from war to peace. He was uncommunicative and withdrawn, restless and prone to outbursts of anger that seemed to come from nowhere. He felt pressure at work, where he had to gear up for a new assignment a few weeks away, a joint training exercise in Africa scheduled for August. "There was little . . . time to process any experiences from Afghanistan because his focus was on a different country," said Liz.[15] He burrowed deeper into his shell, working hard and saying nothing about the inner turmoil. Vivid nightmares robbed him of sleep. He would swing out of bed in the middle of the night, pull on his boots, and walk the perimeter of the base in Stuttgart to make sure the place was secure, just as he had done in Afghanistan. "You could see he had been in the woods all night from the stuff on his boots and pants," said Liz.[16] One night in mid-August, just before he was scheduled to depart for Africa, he barged into the bedroom at one A.M. with a flashlight in his teeth and a suitcase in each hand.

Liz asked what he was doing.

No reply.

She asked again.

No reply.

"Are you ignoring me now?" she asked.

He blew up. "I don't give a fuck about you!" he yelled. "I can't stand the sight of you. I'm leaving."[17]

She calmed her husband, persuaded him to stay, promised to stick with him, and urged him to seek help—to no avail. "Each time I approached Sean about talking to someone—a chaplain, a counselor, a friend—he said he did not have time because he had to get the team ready for the JCET [Joint Combined Exchange Training]. He told me he would talk to someone when he returned from Africa. Our children and I tried to support Sean as best . . . we could with love, hugs, space, and whatever we could do to make him smile and show him how much we loved him."[18]

It was not enough. When he came back from Africa in mid-September, he was in worse shape than when he had left. He drank six beers at a sitting to ease the pain, veering between despondency and rage.[19] He slammed doors and spewed obscenities at his wife and children. Then he felt rotten and blamed himself for pushing them away. He walked past people he knew without acknowledging their presence.[20] He wondered if he was going crazy.[21] "He felt like a failure," Liz said, "like this was his fault, like he was not good enough, like he had let me and his unit down. He was trying to prove . . . that there was nothing wrong with him by taking care of things himself instead of reaching out for help."[22]

As a seasoned medical professional, in his lucid moments Sean suspected that he had PTSD. But he refused to report the illness to superiors for fear that he would be seen as weak and lose his job. "These men are trained to kick down doors and to be resilient," said Liz. "They're not trained to navigate things like PTSD." Her husband did not seek help, "because even in this day and age of the Army, too many people see PTSD as a weakness, something to be ashamed of and something to be hidden. When I urged him to report the problem to his chain of command, he begged me not to. He was so afraid they would put him on a desk job, that it would kill his career, that it would separate him from his men."[23] All this, despite the Army's stated policy that there is no penalty for having PTSD, which is treated as a medical issue. "The word has gone out from the top," said Liz, "but nobody at the working level believes it. There's still a stigma."[24]

As an alternative to treatment within the system, Liz persuaded Sean to seek help from outside channels, first from a social worker, who immediately diagnosed the symptoms of PTSD, then from an Army psychiatrist, who concluded that Sean was suffering from severe depression.[25] The psychiatrist arranged several therapy sessions and prescribed Paxil, the powerful antidepressant often recommended in such cases.[26]

The medication seemed to have little effect. Sean put on a good show at work, where he knew how to answer questionnaires that screened for mental distress. "He was very, very good at hiding things from people and putting up walls to keep them at a distance," said Liz. "Nobody knew what was going on." At home he caromed between gestures of affection and flights of verbal abuse, keeping Liz and the kids off-balance.[27] "His anger could turn on a dime," she said. "He could be livid one minute and apologetic the next."[28]

One of his tender moments came on September 11, 2008, Liz's thirty-seventh birthday, when he presented her with a collection of symbolic gifts—a compass, a whistle, a toy soldier, and a necklace. He told her to use the compass when she felt lost. "We'd helped each other to find our way so many times," she said. If she blew the orange and yellow safety whistle, "he'd be there at my side." The toy soldier was to remind Liz of her soldier and "how much he loved me." The gold necklace was in two pieces with Scripture inscribed on them; they could be read only when the two tablets were together. "The Lord watch between me and thee when we are absent one from another," read the verse, from Genesis 31:49. "He asked if I would wear this necklace as a symbol of us being part of a whole," Liz said.[29]

It was an encouraging episode, but all too brief. By mid-September, Sean's fits of anger grew more frightening. Although he never laid a hand on Liz or the children, he now threatened them with bodily harm. "I'll take you down with me," he said during one tirade. "He started identifying himself as a monster," Liz said. "He told me he was an evil man, that I did not deserve to be with him . . . and that I needed to run away from him as quickly as I could. He said that I needed to get a restraining order against him or he needed to move out." That did it. Concerned about her own safety and that of the children, she reluctantly agreed to separate from Sean in mid-September 2008. She kept the kids in their apartment on base. Sean moved into barracks nearby.[30]

Despite Sean's outbursts, he tried to maintain relations with his family. Every morning, heading for his office just across a field from the building where Liz worked, he would look to her window, and the couple would exchange silent greetings and waves.[31] Every evening he called to wish Hayley and Michael good-night, came by to exchange hugs with them every few days, and made plans to join the family for Thanksgiving in the United States. He continued taking medication and sporadically saw the Army therapist, who never reported his condition to the chain of command.[32] Now unable to concentrate at work, he called Liz during the day and asked for meetings in the woods beside the bowling alley on base. There he poured out his heart about his war experiences in Afghanistan, recalling how frightened he had been while leading nocturnal raids, which had never troubled him before. He cried. He fumed about an officer who detailed Mocabee and his men to pick up cigarette butts at their post in Afghanistan after a particularly dangerous mission, as if they were recruits in boot camp. He apologized profusely for alienating his family. He worried about living alone.

The talks in the woods seemed to calm him, but only temporarily.[33] On three occasions that autumn he felt the urge to kill himself and called Liz for support—once from the railroad tracks, where he planned to jump in front of a train; once from the woods, where he searched for a cliff to leap from; once from a rigging tower, where he looped a rope around his neck and threatened to hang himself. Liz talked him down each time and quietly recruited several of Sean's Army buddies to sound the alarm if he headed for danger.[34]

The friends took Sean out for beers, invited him to watch televised ball games in their homes, and listened to his tales of marital woes. They noticed that Sean, always reserved, was more withdrawn than usual, but he was still functioning, making plans for the future. "Sean seemed to be okay, not depressed but not real upbeat," said one friend. "He did not seem to be bummed out or anything."[35]

Yet he did speak obliquely about suicide. "Sean told me he was thinking the worst," said one of his friends, a warrant officer and former teammate. "I said, 'I know what the worst means, and that is not an option for you,'" the friend said. "I went on to explain that as a father taking the easy way out is not a choice he can make . . . I told him that I see him having two possible courses of action. The best case is that he becomes the person he told me he wants to be . . . and try to be a better father and husband. If so, maybe a year or so down the road Liz would see this and ask him back. The worst case is that he will stay divorced but gets to be a great father to his two kids. Either way he is a winner. He agreed but I could tell he wasn't completely satisfied. He wanted to be with his family."[36]

At the next sign of trouble, Liz resolved to bundle Sean off to the hospital—against his will if necessary.[37] She never got the chance. He phoned the kids for their routine good-night call on Sunday, November 9, and made plans to meet the family on November 11, when both parents had the day off for Veterans Day. He called again a few minutes later, got Liz on the line, and said, "You win." Then he hung up.[38]

At some point between that call and the morning of Wednesday, November 12, he retreated to his private room on base, knotted a nylon strap to the clothes bar of a closet, and hanged himself. When he failed to report for the morning training formation on Wednesday, November 12, First Sgt. Chris Lofgrin and another soldier got a master key and entered Sean's room, where he was hanging, half-sitting and half-standing, a few inches above a chair in a corner closet. They cut him down, a medic was summoned, and they dragged Sean out into his room to check for vital signs. There were none. His face was so swollen that he was hardly recognizable. He had been dead for at least eight hours, probably longer. On his desk was a Paxil bottle with nine pills inside, a full serving of German beer in a Mickey Mouse glass, a plate of cheese and sausage, and a book, *Breaking the Chain of Low Self-Esteem*, by Marilyn J. Sorenson.[39]

He left no suicide note. Most people never do.[40] But looking back on her husband's last moments, Liz felt that his enigmatic parting shot, "You win," served as one. "That short, one-sided conversation I now believe was his suicide note," she said. "Sean wavered between feeling like the world was out to get him and clinging to our children and me so he would not feel so alone. When he said 'You win,' I strongly suspect he was feeling like the world was after him, myself included, and just gave up."[41]

In the hours following her husband's death, Liz made the difficult round of telephone calls to the family, tried to explain things to her children, and began making arrangements for Sean's funeral at Arlington, which he had designated as his preferred place of burial before deploying to Afghanistan.[42] Investigators sifted through evidence from Sean's apartment, interviewed colleagues and family, and ruled his death a suicide. Looking through the investigative reports, it is striking in hindsight how so many people saw signs of trouble but so few could help him.[43]

He had deftly masked his intentions in sessions with an Army psychiatrist, who completely misjudged her patient.

The doctor, a lieutenant colonel whose name was redacted from investigative reports, told military police after Sean's death that he "was the last one she would have thought of committing suicide." Even though he spoke of killing himself, the doctor told investigators that she could not commit him "to a treatment facility unless she was aware of an incident taking place or he made it known that he wasn't going to call for help if these thoughts came up again* . . . As long as the service member says he isn't going to carry out the suicidal act or says he will call for help if the thoughts come up, then the hospital will not admit him for in-patient care." After three sessions over a one-month period, the psychiatrist had released Sean without any restrictions and asked him to come back for a fourth treatment session. He never did.[44]

The violent nature of Mocabee's death went unmentioned when he came home for final honors at Arlington on December 5, 2008, a cold, bright day that sent winds racing over the cemetery, rattled the trees, and made the flags snap. Friends and family converged on the Old Post Chapel at Fort Myer, a mellow redbrick building with a soaring white steeple that guards the cemetery gates by Meigs Drive.

For those who knew Sean, it was an unsettling moment when a solider in dress greens rose from the front pew, passed the flag-covered casket at the front of the church, and mounted the steps to the pulpit. It was as if a ghost had appeared: with his fringe of close-clipped red hair, dimpled grin, and military bearing, Army Capt. Rob Mocabee might have been his brother's stunt double, a younger version of the man he had come to eulogize.[45]

---

* This puzzling statement suggests that the doctor was not aware of her patient's intention to take his own life, even though he had threatened to kill himself on at least three occasions. She knew about these incidents but did not consider them serious enough to hospitalize her patient.

"Sean was always my hero," said Rob, a Chinook helicopter pilot with years of combat experience. "I always used to tag along. He went before me and experienced things first. I watched him and learned, and sometimes I found myself in the same kind of trouble."[46]

Rob, who dreamed of being a Ranger, recalled how he had begun to doubt his own ability to complete the grueling training course. He had called Sean for advice. "He didn't coddle me," Rob said. "In no uncertain terms he told me to stop whining and just do it. He followed that up with an encouraging letter in which he enclosed a simple piece of cloth and told me to stay focused on my goal. Today that piece of cloth is right here." He tapped the black and gold Ranger tab on his left shoulder. "I will always wear it. I don't care how tattered it gets. It's there due in no small part to his mentorship."[47]

Rob paused to compose himself. "Sean gave his life for his country," he said. "He went to places none of us will go and experienced things none of us can imagine. He died in combat, and he will be in this home of heroes at Arlington. He is a hero too." He nodded toward his brother's casket. "I will see you someday," he said. "For now, good-bye brother."[48]

Emerging from the chapel into the sunlight, the funeral party made its way down the long, winding drive past Robert E. Lee's old mansion, past thousands of faded tombstones from Civil War days, past all the dead from all the wars since then, and down through the avenue of trees to the business end of Section 60, where hardly a week passed without new burials.

Arriving on York Drive, the eight-man casket team from the Old Guard lined up behind a black hearse, eased the flag-draped casket out of the car, executed a measured five-step turn, and slow-marched Sean Mocabee across the grass to a fresh gravesite, where cemetery workers had spread mats over the muddy ground and set out folding chairs draped with green velvet covers for the family. The family, bundled in overcoats and mufflers against the cold, took their places, whereupon a handful of Sean's Special Forces comrades, hard-looking men bristling medals, edged into position around the family and braced themselves, some streaming tears as the casket team lifted the flag and held it taut over a brother whose long war had finally ended.

A civilian minister read from the Bible, murmured the time-worn words of comfort, and stepped back. The Old Guard's firing party stiffened, brandished their rifles, and let loose three volleys. The smoke still hung over the crowd as the bugler began Taps, which rang sharp and clear on the wintry air. While Liz hugged her daughter Hayley close, the casket team began their slow, deliberate ritual, folding the flag into a triangle and passing it to a senior Green Beret, who stepped across the grass, knelt on one knee, and offered the flag to Liz Mocabee:

"On behalf of the President of the United States, the United States Army, and a grateful nation," he said, "please accept this flag as a symbol of our appreciation for your loved one's honor-able and faithful service." He stood, snapped off a salute, and turned back to the grave. The service was finished. Liz stood alone, gently placed five red roses on Sean's casket, and leaned over to kiss the polished wooden box[49] that held the man she still considered her "best friend, the love of my life . . . lost to something called PTSD."[50]

Years after Sean's death, his oldest friends still struggled to understand what had happened to one of the smartest and most durable soldiers they had known.

"It hit me like a piano dropping on my head," said Glenn Oliver, the long-retired master sergeant who had trained with Sean as a Green Beret. "I wish he had reached out to me— maybe I could've helped. One underlying problem is that the Special Forces boys are all type A. We can't show any weakness. 'Pop a Motrin and carry on,' that's our motto. Most of the guys still think that it's a career-ending move to announce you're having problems. I can totally see that, and I can totally see why Sean tried to hide it. He would know just what to say—all the medics do. But it's still a shock. I never pictured him doing something like this."[51]

David Hill was just as surprised. "Last time I saw Sean was in Kabul," Hill said. "He was bringing his team out of Afghanistan, I was bringing mine in, and we stood on the ramp of a C-120 and talked for a few minutes. We joked about being old guys with twenty years in, ready to quit. I was like 'What are you doing here? I thought you were retiring,' and we just laughed it off. He looked okay. I mean I had no idea there was anything going on with him. The next thing I knew he was dead. It was a complete shock."[52]

Hill, a trim, compact man in a Red Sox cap, made his way across Section 60 on a recent spring morning. He limped slightly, picking his way among the tight-knit community of special ops friends claimed by the recent wars: Maj. Jeffrey Philip "Toz" Toczylowski, thirty, who fell out of a chopper in Iraq; Master Sgt. Thomas D. Maholic, thirty-eight, shot by insurgents in Kandahar Province, Afghanistan; Sgt. Maj. Bradley D. Conner, forty-one, blown up by an improvised explosive device in Iraq; Master Sgt. Anthony "Tony" Ray Charles Yost, a larger-than-life Native American inevitably known to Army pals as "Chief."[53]

"This one was a big, scary guy," said Hill, pausing before Yost's tombstone, which was inscribed with a teepee. "He rode a red Harley, went skydiving, went to the bars, then to the gym, full-throttle all the way. He had to be out front." Hill recalled the combat action that finally claimed his friend. "There was this big firefight in Mosul, Iraq, 2005. He was leading Iraqi soldiers into a house where the bad guys had barricaded. They were searching for Abu Musab al-Zarqawi [leader of Al Qaeda in Iraq]. So the bullets are flying, and then there's a huge explosion that leveled the house. Tony's right in the middle of it. I wasn't there, but his wife later asked me to look at his autopsy pictures to see what killed him. The official story was that he died from the blast, but I counted four wounds, one of which I'm pretty sure was fatal." For his actions that day, Anthony Ray Charles Yost received the Silver Star posthumously, the Army's third-highest award for valor.[54]

Hill came to Sean's grave, which is situated near the middle of Section 60. Like others in the special ops fraternity, Hill felt intense camaraderie with those who shared the danger he had known for years at war—kicking down doors, chasing the bad guys, living on the edge where a fraction of an inch or an extra minute made the difference between a life lost and a life saved. Having just moved from that adrenaline-fueled milieu to one characterized by the meetings and daily PowerPoint presentations at the Pentagon, where Hill now worked as a civilian, he sorely missed the soldier's life. He wondered if Sean, too, felt lost between two worlds, with his family ties strained to the breaking point and his military retirement looming. "Who knows what he was thinking?" said Hill. "He probably came to an understanding that he wasn't going to be part of this community anymore. I mean, no more jumping out of airplanes, no more seeing amazing sights, no more going to stinky places that are incredible beyond anything you've ever seen in a movie. Maybe he didn't want to leave that life. I don't know. He fucked up. He knows he fucked up. Now he's left a wife with no husband and two kids with no father." He shook his head and stared at Grave No. 60-8608.[55]

In the aftermath of Sean's suicide, Liz lavished attention on Hayley and Michael, helping them come to terms with their father's death and slowly pulling the family back together. Michael, diagnosed with Asperger's Syndrome, needed special treatment and a good deal of patience with schoolwork, but he has developed into a lively, mischievous boy who meets strangers with a steady gaze and a firm handshake. Hayley, who was particularly angry for two years after her father's death, refused to mention his name or to join her family on regular visits to Section 60 from their new home in California. Now, after counseling and the solid support of her mother, she looks forward to family visits to Washington, D.C., places seashells on her father's grave, and asks for time to sit alone with him at Arlington.[56] She posts heartfelt messages on his Facebook page, where friends and family maintain a link with the departed warrior. "Hey Daddy, with all the gnarliness going on around here, I just remembered your birthday," Hayley wrote in a January 2013 post. "But NO WORRIES, I still totally love you and miss you and hope you have a BANGING party up there in Heaven. Save space for me one day, but for now I made peanut butter chocolate cupcakes to celebrate :) Love you xoxo."[57]

It has been excruciating, but Liz has finally made peace with herself, edged out from under the guilt that shadowed her for so long, and smoothed the kids back into the routines of school and home. She has "worked through just about every piece of pain, sorrow, and baggage I carried when Sean died." How did she do it? "In the beginning it was literally a minute at a time. I wrote a list to follow each day. Get out of bed. Eat breakfast. Write in my journal. Pray. Get the kids up. Feed the kids," and so on. "Every tiny thing that needed to happen was on that list. Slowly things moved from a minute at a time to an hour at a time, then a day at a time. With counseling, through getting the kids the support they needed to heal, drawing on my coun-selor training, and for me, most important, my faith is what got me through. The first couple of years I did a poor job of taking care of me, as I was so focused on keeping the kids in a space that they could heal as much as possible. As their

Michael, Hayley, and Liz Mocabee on one of their regular pilgrimages to Arlington. (Mocabee family photo)

struggles lessened, I started taking better care of myself, which of course helped us all. The progress has been methodical and hard-earned."[58]

Liz and others who have lived with PTSD believe that it is essential for people suffering from the ailment to talk about it, as well as for the families riding the emotional waves set in motion by the psychic trauma. "We're talking to you," she told a writer, "because the kids and I agreed that it might help other families struggling with a loved one's PTSD.[59] There should be no stigma. If you get PTSD, it's like breaking your leg. You get it fixed, but only if you are willing to accept help from someone."[60]

A cemetery seems a strange place to go for therapy, but Section 60 serves that purpose for wounded warriors and their families.[61] "One of the hallmarks of PTSD is avoidance," said Air Force Lt. Col. Pamela Novy, a clinical psychologist who has made Arlington a regular part of her therapy program for active-duty service members. "Almost all of our patients are apprehensive about going to Arlington. They don't want to talk about the trauma. They don't want to dream about it. They don't want to think about it. It's so painful."[62]

Even so, she reminds patients that they are stronger than they think, bundles them into a van for the trip from Walter Reed Army Medical Center, and begins her tours of Arlington at the Tomb of the Unknowns. The precision and ritual of the ceremony there, high on a hill at the heart of the cemetery, reminds her patients of the grand military tradition they are part of and shows that the nation remembers those who served. "They usually leave that part of the cemetery with a renewed sense of pride," said Novy, who then takes them on a walk through Section 60, among the tombstones of comrades killed in Iraq and Afghanistan. "Seeing the tombstones acts as a prompt," she said. "People have been holding their emotions in check because they had missions to complete or wanted to avoid painful memories. When they come to Arlington, they start talking about what happened to them and their friends—very specifically. They tell stories to each other. A lot of them cry, but it's cathartic, and it's the first stage of the healing process. They usually feel better for it."[63]

One former Marine corporal who still makes regular visits to Section 60 is Chase Martin, twenty-seven, a machine gunner who served in Afghanistan and Iraq until he was severely wounded by an IED in Fallujah in 2006. Martin's left arm was almost severed by the blast, which consigned him to more than thirty surgeries, as well as the nightmares, flashbacks, anxiety, and hypervigilance associated with PTSD.[64]

"It actually helps to come here," said Martin, now a senior in Russian studies at American University in Washington, with big plans for the future. "These guys don't have a voice anymore," he said on a recent May morning, walking among the tombstones, "so it's up to those of us who are still here to remember."[65]

Cpl. Chase Martin in Section 60, with a tattoo immortalizing the war injury that nearly took his arm. (Bruce Dale)

Martin might have ended on the wrong side of the turf at Arlington if not for a pair of fast-thinking comrades who dragged him out of harm's way and wrapped his badly mangled arm in a tourniquet in November 2006. He had already lost more than half his blood by the time they stanched the flow. "I was so cold, and it was harder and harder to breathe, I'd lost so much blood," he recalled. "They kept pressure on the wound until I could get out." Martin pleaded with doctors not to amputate his arm, lied to them about feeling sensations in his hand, and slowly, painstakingly regained about 30 percent of the function in his injured limb.[66]

The psychic injuries took longer to heal. They still haunt Martin on occasion, but with therapy and the passage of time, he has learned to manage the worst episodes. He flexed his fingers to show how they still worked and rolled up his sleeve to reveal a neatly rendered tattoo of a tourniquet on his left bicep, commemorating his near-death experience in Fallujah. The tattoo is a permanent tribute to the Marines who saved him and a reminder of the random recruitment process for Section 60. "Dumb luck, no question about it." Martin looked around at the ocean of tombstones. "It's just dumb luck."[67]

For Martin and others who seek help for PTSD, the journey to recovery is seldom easy, but the results are usually worth the investment. After more than a decade of tragic trial and error, mental health professionals have improved treatment regimens for PTSD and associated injuries, with outcomes that are far from perfect but nonetheless encouraging. Now the Army claims that 80 percent of its soldiers diagnosed with PTSD are healthy enough to remain on active duty, while the remaining 20 percent are medically discharged and entrusted to the Veterans Administration for treatment.[68]

"It doesn't have to be a death sentence," said Fred Gusman, a Vietnam-era veteran and social worker who helped pioneer treatment for PTSD at Veterans Administration hospitals in the San Francisco Bay Area. Gusman now oversees an innovative private treatment center called The Pathway Home, in Yountville, California, where trauma sessions, in which participants are encouraged to relate their wartime experiences, are the heart of the program. Gusman's regime also includes anger management, yoga, and acupuncture. And to help warriors ward off their feelings of isolation, Gusman leads his troops on forays into the civilian world of the Napa Valley for bowling, fly-fishing, bike rides, and meals. "The real test is when they go outside," said Gusman. "That's why we encourage them to get out into the community . . . They have to figure out why they're angry or anxious and unravel it. We give them the tools to realize when they're spinning and need to stop. They learn to modulate their emotions."[69]

In some instances, however, no amount of love, patience, or innovative therapy is strong enough to break the grip of PTSD, which followed Marine Cpl. Eric W. Hall home from

Cpl. Eric Hall in Iraq. (Hall family photo)

Iraq, stalked him for two and a half years, and finally dispatched him to Arlington National Cemetery, where he lies within shouting distance of Sean Mocabee's grave.

Age twenty-one when he arrived in Iraq with the First Battalion of the Sixth Marine Regiment, Hall had already seen action in Afghanistan and earned his position as a squad leader. In 2005 he plunged into the bitterly contested fight for Anbar Province in June of that year, leading young Marines and Iraqi allies on patrol through the densely packed streets. He stepped off a curb and felt the world implode around him. Someone had set off an improvised explosive device, producing a massive blast that sent up clouds of dust, ripped through parked cars, and propelled fragments of metal in all directions.[70] Hall, knocked off his feet by the force of the explosion, saw his friend Pfc. Joshua P. Klinger, twenty-one, a recent recruit on his first combat tour, decapitated beside him. Hall tried to stand but could not. The bomb had crushed his left femur and shredded his leg.

He remained conscious throughout the ordeal, which eventually landed him in Bethesda Naval Medical Center outside

Washington. There he would spend months fighting his way back, struggling to overcome pneumonia and a virulent infection called *Acinetobacter*, which resists standard antibiotics and is treated with a chemotherapy drug. Surgeons pieced Hall's mangled leg back together, using a metal rod to replace part of his shattered femur, grafting muscle from his abdomen to fashion new quadriceps, and borrowing skin from his right leg to cover the wound. For persistent pain, he was kept heavily medicated, which may have acerbated his nightmares and hallucinations—of gun barrels popping from the walls, floors bathed in blood, bugs and spiders swarming over his arms and legs, insurgents pressing close for an attack. After one surgery, he woke up convinced that he was a prisoner of war and had to be restrained, which only made matters worse.[71]

"This kid's leg was about half gone," said Hall's father, Kevin, a maintenance supervisor at the courthouse in Jeffersonville, Indiana, who kept vigil with his wife, Becky, through Eric's long hospital odyssey. "We were so focused on keeping him alive and saving his leg—that was the main problem—until this high-ranking psychiatrist pulled me aside one day and said, 'Don't worry about the physical injuries. He'll overcome those. Worry about PTSD.' That's the first time I ever heard of PTSD." Kevin was puzzled by the psychiatrist's comment. "I'm thinking, 'Man, you just don't understand what's going on here!'"

In truth, as Kevin Hall now acknowledges, the shrink's prognosis proved to be uncannily accurate. "He had it just right," said Kevin. "Eric got over the worst of the physical issues, but the real problem was just beginning."

With his leg patched together but not yet functional, Eric Hall was sent home to recuperate, armed with enough OxyContin to last 270 days. "He was in a lot of pain," said his mother, Becky, "and they treated it very aggressively." He developed an addiction to the painkillers, hobbled around, and slowly regained strength in his injured limb. But the proud Marine who had seemed so invincible had come home to Indiana transformed—worried, anxious, frightened, and broken, a ghost of the young man who had so boldly marched off to war a few years before.

"The first time I noticed something was wrong," said Kevin, "was when we went out to the range to shoot clay targets. Eric had always been very good at it, and he enjoyed doing it." After firing three rounds out of the usual twenty-five volleys, Eric panicked and asked to go home. "I didn't question him," said Kevin. "We got in the car. He wouldn't say anything. Then about halfway home he said, 'Dad, I got to tell you that the smell of that gunpowder, it just flashed me back so bad.'" The stimulus transported him to the war zone, which he continued to visit in nightmares. "He'd wake up screaming and drenched in sweat," said Becky.

Diagnosed with PTSD, he slept with a pistol and swerved his car around manhole covers he believed to be planted with IEDs. He screeched to a halt for roadblocks that were not there. He felt he was being followed by insurgents in traffic, accelerated to evade them, and tried to hide from them behind Dumpsters. "He was doing what you do to stay alive down-range," said Chaz Kane, a first cousin and airman with whom Eric was particularly close.

Such behavior is, of course, considered threatening in the civilian world, which landed Eric in trouble on occasion. A judge yanked his license to carry a handgun after he pulled the weapon during a traffic altercation. His dependence on pain-killers increased even as his leg mended. He gulped OxyContin, along with Xanax, an antianxiety drug prescribed for his PTSD. He entered a month-long detoxification program aimed at weaning him from painkillers. He returned to Bethesda to have the metal rod removed from his left leg, which remained shorter than his right one, giving him a permanent limp. Medically discharged from the Marines, he returned home to Indiana in 2007. He seemed better for a spell but then spiraled into depression, haunted by recurring memories of the brutalities he had seen—and committed—in wartime.

He told family members he had been forced to kill children in Iraq, where youths were often recruited as suicide bombers or gunmen for the enemy. "The kids would plant the IEDs," said Justin Hall, Eric's older brother and a recent Navy veteran. "A kid would be walking down the street with a gun, and he wouldn't stop. They'd just have to blast them. That's what fucked Eric up."

Eric also blamed himself for the death of his friend Pfc. Joshua Klinger, whom he had promised to protect. "The last thing Eric told Klinger's mom before they got on the bus for Iraq was that he would take care of him," said Kevin.

"The guilt just ate him up," said Becky. "He never forgave himself. What he had to do in Iraq and Afghanistan went against everything he'd been raised to do, all the killing you had to do or the shot you had to take or the guy you lost. When you're debilitated and your psyche isn't all that it should be, it eats at you. I think the combination just overwhelmed Eric. He loved the Marine Corps. He was so proud of that uniform. But he lost that too. One day he looked right at me and said, 'Mom, the Marine Corps doesn't want me anymore. I'm broke and they don't want me.' That's what he said."

At his lowest point, beaten down by a harsh winter in Indiana, Eric admitted to his father that he was afraid of dying. "I don't know if it was going to be at the hands of imaginary Iraqis or from somewhere else, but he thought he was going to die," said Kevin. "He just had the feeling that something bad was going to happen to him. We hung in there, but we could only take it so far."

Hoping that a change of scene would improve his situation, Eric accepted an offer to visit his cousin Chaz Kane and other relatives in Deep Creek, Florida. He moved there in January 2008, bunked in Kane's apartment, buzzed around the strip malls and scrub brush on his blue Yamaha motorcycle, and talked about looking for work. "He was doing all right," Kane recalled. "One of his big issues was weaning himself off the meds. I said, 'Okay, we'll slowly take you down.' But he wanted to do it cold turkey. He really didn't talk much about the past, but it seemed like he was getting better at socializing and stuff like that. When he went off the meds, though—pain and antianxiety—that's when some of the problems started again."[72]

His fretfulness spiked, and his insomnia worsened. He was sleeping a couple of hours at night, wandering and watchful the rest of the time. His flashbacks multiplied. On the morning of Super Bowl Sunday, February 3, 2008, Chaz and Eric were sitting together while Chaz played a video game in his apartment. Eric began speaking incoherent military jargon into an imaginary microphone on his left shoulder.

"Are you all right, cousin?" Chaz asked, looking up from his computer.

"I'm good," said Eric. But then he resumed the chatter a moment later, speaking to his shoulder.

"Are you sure you're okay?" Chaz asked.

"Yes," Eric answered. "Are you okay?"

Minutes after that, Eric stood and announced that he was taking his motorcycle for a spin, and the cousins agreed to meet later at Chaz's mother's house for a Super Bowl dinner with their grandmother, who was visiting from out of town.

"That was the last time I saw him," said Chaz.[73]

About two hours after that, their grandmother called Chaz from his mother's house. "Grandma was hysterical," Chaz said. Eric had come unhinged. He jabbered to people who were not there, going from window to window to look for insurgents marshaling around the house. He ordered his grandmother to lie on the floor to avoid getting shot. He set a pillow on fire, stomped out the blaze, ran outside, and roared off on his motorcycle.[74]

Police found his blue Yamaha a mile or so down the road near Harbor Heights, still running with the keys in the ignition. The bike was laid on its side in a low area of scrub grass and palmettos, a landscape eerily evocative of the one Eric Hall had known in Iraq. He was nowhere to be seen. The half-acre around his bike had been scorched by a brush fire. The blaze, which fire crews had quickly doused, melted Eric's motorcycle helmet, which was found near his bike. Deputies mounted a search with helicopters, horses, and cadaver dogs—to no avail. They gave up after a week of scouring nearby creeks and scrublands, whereupon the search was taken over by Becky Hall, other relatives, and scores of perfect strangers who poured into southwestern Florida to look for the missing Marine.[75]

"We weren't going to just let him be gone and not find him, so we put our own search party together," said Becky. "Justin was there. Chaz was there. Kevin stayed at home in Indiana in case Eric tried to call him. We had airplanes, helicopters, dogs, and boats combing up and down the harbors. Four wheelers. Divers in the canals with the alligators. We handed out flyers and searched every square inch of that country."[76]

As word of Eric's disappearance spread, it struck a chord with a ragtag band of old Marines who lived in the area— Charlie Shaughnessy, Jerry "Animal" Lutz, and Thomas "Wolf" McCarthy, all Vietnam veterans who soon joined the search for a missing brother. They may have seen something of themselves in the restless young man they had never met but knew very well. Long before PTSD was recognized, they too had fought their own battles with the disorder, clawed their way back to some semblance of normalcy, and settled in

South Florida. Shaughnessy and McCarthy in particular obsessed over Eric, crashed into the scrub day after day, rumbled through the harsh terrain on four-wheelers, interrogated the inhabitants of homeless camps, and bumped over miles of narrow dirt roads in McCarthy's silver pickup truck looking for some hint that Eric had been there. It gave them something important to do—a mission.[77]

Five weeks after Eric's disappearance, Shaughnessy returned to the area where the Marine's bike had been found. Arming himself with a knife and a flashlight, he wriggled into a nearby metal culvert, which wafted the unmistakable scent of decomposing flesh. Hoping the smell came from an old raccoon or another luckless critter, Shaughnessy crawled twenty-five yards into the pipe, where from the gloom his flashlight beam picked out the pale profile of a human skull and jaw.[78]

He backed out of the culvert and into the sun—and turned around to find Becky Hall waiting for him.

"Is it Eric?" she asked, knowing the answer before Shaughnessy said a word.[79]

A few days later Eric's remains were identified from dental records and from his voluminously documented surgical history. But some mystery remained: after more than a month in the heat and humidity of the Gulf Coast, his advanced state of decomposition made it impossible to establish exactly what killed him. "Undetermined" was the one-word verdict of the Charlotte County medical examiner.[80]

"They thought he died in the fire," said Becky. "It appears that he had backed himself into that drainage tile to get away from it. And because the pipe was closed off at the other end, he couldn't get out." Witnesses later established that Eric had ditched his bike as one car approached him from behind and another came toward him—in his mind, perhaps, the setup for an ambush by enemies. He ran from the danger and took cover, possibly setting the brush fire to divert his imaginary pursuers. For her part, Becky Hall thought the blaze was accidental. "I'm certain beyond a doubt that he flipped a cigarette down, not thinking of how dry it is in Florida in February," she said. "I think he was just trying to get away from the fire or trying to get away from the Iraqis when he went into that tile."[81]

Given the state of Eric's remains, his family decided to cremate their son. His newest Marine pals, Shaughnessy and McCarthy, insisted on driving his ashes from Florida to Indiana, a final gesture of solidarity from one generation to the next. "After all they had been through with Eric," said Kevin Hall, "those guys wouldn't think of leaving that job to anybody else. I just wish Eric had known them. They had been through the same stuff, and they might have helped him. If he had just talked to them . . ."[82]

After funeral services in Florida and Indiana, the last stage of Eric W. Hall's long, eventful journey ended in Section 60 of Arlington on June 27, 2008. There Marine Corps comrades, resplendent in their dress-blue coats, snow-white trousers, and white gloves, received him in grand style. They tenderly bore him to his grave to the familiar clatter of rifle fire and the calming strains of Taps, which settled over one of their own, sleeping at last.

5

IMPROVISED DEATH

T HE MARINES TAKE care of their own. So there was not a
moment's doubt that Jim and Alison Malachowski would
drive the nine hours from their home in Westminster,
Maryland, to the snowbound hills of Danville, Vermont, for
the funeral of Cpl. Ian M. Muller, a friend and comrade of
their son, Staff Sgt. Jimmy Malachowski.

The younger Malachowski, Muller's platoon sergeant at
Patrol Base Dakota near Marjah, Afghanistan, had helped
recover the young Vermonter's body after he was killed by
an improvised explosive device on March 11, 2011. "Because
Jimmy had asked us to represent him at Ian's funeral, we
got in the car and went—no questions asked," said his
mother, Alison, herself a retired Marine sergeant who
understood the importance of showing up for such
occasions.[1]

Following Muller's funeral, which was flooded by hundreds
of neighbors and friends from his tight-knit New England

Staff Sgt. Jimmy Malachowski mingles with children in Afghanistan.
(Malachowski family photo)

community, the Malachowskis returned home to Maryland on March 20, worn out by their trip. To loosen up from the long drive and get ready for spring, Alison, an avid gardener, went to work in the yard, moving bulbs and digging in the fragrant earth. She relished the end of another winter and looked forward to her son's return with summer. "I wanted everything to look good for Jimmy," she said. "I was out there to make sure we'd have flowers for him."[2]

As she knelt in the dirt, she noticed movement out of the corner of her eye, a gray van with government plates creeping up the driveway. When it came to a stop, two officers emerged, a Marine first sergeant and an Army captain, both dressed in formal rig. They strode over to Alison, who noticed that the captain was a chaplain. She scuttled away from them. They caught up and told her that Jimmy Malachowski had been killed in Afghanistan a few hours earlier, another IED casualty, not far from where Ian Muller had been blown up just nine days before. "No, Jimmy's not dead," said his mother. "I know he's alive. He's alive!" She turned her back on the officers. Realizing the futility of their mission, the men reversed course with a plan to return the next day. Even as the van disappeared down the drive, Alison felt the dreadful reality sink in: her only son would never see another summer.[3]

This was confirmed the next day when the gray van returned and Marine First Sgt. Evan A. Good and Army Capt. Shawn D. Hunze briefed the Malachowskis on the circumstances of their son's death and helped them make plans for his funeral at Arlington. Like many others laid to rest there in recent years, Malachowski had been killed by a homemade bomb, one of many variants of the cheap, powerful weapon similar to those that would wreak havoc at the Boston Marathon in 2013, and one responsible for killing or maiming more allied combatants than any other weapon in Iraq and Afghanistan.[4]

The IED that claimed Malachowski had been buried under the dirt floor of an abandoned farmhouse where he and other Marines had planned to meet Hajji Gul Mala, a charismatic local leader from Marjah, on March 20. Gul Mala, a lifelong resident of northern Helmand Province, had assembled and armed his own militia to maintain local order and to repel the Taliban, which had bullied and threatened villagers for years. His new private army, financed with funds the Marines had provided, was one of many local militias known as Interim Security for Critical Infrastructure (ISCI), units organized to help the United States and coalition forces. The buildup of ISCI combatants coincided with the surge of thirty thousand fresh U.S. troops in 2010 and 2011, aimed at shifting the war's momentum.[5]

Malachowski, a veteran of three previous deployments to Iraq, had no illusions about the dangers of operating in this battered corner of southern Afghanistan, where the Second Battalion of the Ninth Marine Regiment had established the first Patrol Base Dakota in 2010, only to have the outpost destroyed by heavy Taliban fire. Malachowski's unit, the Second Battalion of the Eighth Marines, had taken over in

Sgt. Tom Whorl, Staff Sgt. Jimmy Malachowski, and Cpl. Ian Muller in Helmand Province, hours before Muller was killed there.
(Navy Corpsman Jesse "Doc" Deller)

January 2011, rebuilt the base, and braced for the spring fighting season.[6]

"This may turn out to be an eventful deployment," he wrote his parents that winter. "The Taliban are all training in Pakistan right now but they will be back soon . . . Anyway everyone is doing well here. We have a generator and a thatch roof over our heads so we can't complain."[7]

Over countless cups of tea and many discussions, Malachowski and Sgt. Tom Whorl, his squad leader, forged an alliance with Gul Mala, who reopened a local school, helped Marines identify insurgents, and eagerly joined the fight against the Taliban. Of Gul Mala and his militia, Malachowski wrote, "They are a tribal gang for the most part that hate the Taliban."[8]

About twenty of Gul Mala's ISCI troops joined the Marines in patrolling the dry, dusty countryside, gathering intelligence and engaging the adversary. Malachowski was impressed by the performance not only of his own troops but also of his Afghan allies. "Let me tell you we are kicking ass," Malachowski crowed to his sister Brandy, then an Army lieutenant and a veteran of the Iraq War, as the fighting season commenced.[9] He expressed grudging respect for the elusive Taliban. "They even dress up like women and shoot at us so we can't find them!!" Malachowski wrote. "Sneaky Taliban. I have never been shot at by a man dressed in women's clothing before . . . I got to sprint about 800 m[eters] down a road under fire. Talk about exhilarating!"[10]

On the day before he died, Malachowski reported an instance of rough justice on the Afghan front: his joint patrol team had tracked down and killed Ian Muller's assassin, an insurgent bomb maker named Makeem, in a firefight. They also detained five Taliban suspects, wounded others, discovered a cache of IED-making supplies, and called air strikes on enemy positions. "The ISCI love us, the locals say they feel safer," wrote the twenty-five-year-old Malachowski, whose own death was hours away, most likely from the workshop of the Talib fighter his Marines had just killed.[11]

Villagers, Marines, and members of the local militia converged on a mud-walled compound in northern Marjah on March 20, when the new allies planned to establish Gul Mala's headquarters. They set up a makeshift flagpole on the roof and hoisted the Afghan colors, a rebuke to Taliban struggling to control the region. Lt. Col. John D. Harrill, commander of Second Battalion of the Eighth Marine Regiment, made the trek up from battalion headquarters, along with several members of his staff, to demonstrate his commitment to local allies.[12]

Members of Malachowski's platoon ducked inside the mud-walled building to make a final check for hidden IEDs. Sgt. Tom Whorl and Cpl. Craig Fazenbaker swept the rooms with mine detectors, while Lance Cpl. Matthew Westbrook went through with Holly, a yellow Labrador trained to sniff bombs. The inspection done, Whorl radioed Malachowski: "Building clear, building clear."[13]

At that, Gul Mala filed in with Colonel Harrill and his reti-
nue, along with Malachowski, who stood against an inside
wall to watch the meeting unfold. Tom Whorl and other
platoon members positioned themselves outside, on the look-
out for suspicious activity. Inside, Malachowski may have
shifted his weight at one point, fatefully pressing his two-
hundred-pound bulk on an IED trigger undetected by the
sweep. He set off a tremendous blast that shook the building,
sent dust and shrapnel ripping through the air, and nearly cut
Malachowski in half at the waist. The lieutenant colonel and
two other Marines staggered out of the smoke and into the
sunlight, bleeding from wounds to their faces and backs. Gul
Mala, also stunned by the blast, wobbled out on his own
steam. Sergeant Whorl, knocked flat but grasping the gravity
of the situation, immediately radioed for a medevac chopper
and rushed to aid Malachowski, who was still conscious and
calling for the sergeant.[14]

With Navy Corpsman Jesse "Doc" Deller, Whorl frantically
tried to stop Malachowski's bleeding, which was too high on his
legs for tourniquets to be effective. Whorl reassured Malachowski
that help was on the way and that things would be all right,
although he almost certainly knew his friend was beyond help.
Deller began CPR. Comrades settled Malachowski onto a
stretcher, carried him to a nearby field where a landing zone had
been cleared, and listened for the *thump-thump-thump* of the
approaching helicopter. As they waited, Whorl watched
Malachowski go pale as his life drained away into the unforgiv-
ing soil of Helmand Province, which had already claimed more
than its fair share of Marines. "He just bled out—there was
nothing we could do," Whorl said.[15]

Why, after the sweep with two mine detectors and a bomb-
sniffing dog, had the lethal IED gone undiscovered? A
follow-up investigation suggested that it was because the bomb

maker had used hardly any metal in the device, except for two paper-thin strips in its trigger plate and in the wires running to a plastic jug containing fifteen pounds of ammonium nitrate crystals, the explosive most often used in such bombs.[16]

Simple to make, inexpensive to assemble, and hard to detect, IEDs had taken a staggering toll on U.S. and coalition troops in Iraq and Afghanistan by October 2013, killing 2,527 combatants—this, despite Herculean efforts to foil the signature weapon of our most recent wars.[17]

The IED is nothing new; indeed, its triple-barreled name comes from the 1970s, when British soldiers in Northern Ireland were bedeviled by similar explosives. Homemade bombs also took their toll in World War II, when partisans deployed them against Germans; in Vietnam, where they were known as booby traps; and in Oklahoma City, where in 1995 Timothy McVeigh and others set off a massive truck bomb killing 168 people at a federal office building.[18]

Notwithstanding this history, U.S. military planners failed to anticipate the threat of IEDs in the rush to war with Iraq in 2003. Troops lacked effective body armor, trucks were poorly shielded against explosives, and combatants were inadequately trained to spot hidden roadside bombs. Young men and women were soon coming home in pieces for the first funerals at Arlington, where IED casualties would continue to fill new graves.[19]

Combatants scrambled to counter IEDs on the fighting front by armoring flimsy Humvees with sandbags and sheet metal. Those who could afford to buy armored vests from private suppliers did so with their own money. Military leaders, prodded by Congress, responded with an ambitious program to thwart the IED menace. A year into the Iraq War, this program, grandly styled the Joint Improvised Explosive Device Defeat Organization, or JIEDDO, employed more than nineteen hundred people, launched a flurry of research, and spent \$21 billion, surpassing the Manhattan Project of World War II in its outlay of inflation-adjusted dollars, but with poorer results.[20]

In one well-publicized JIEDDO project, bees were transported to the Los Alamos National Laboratory in New Mexico and trained to detect explosives. This \$2 million program, called the Stealthy Insect Sensor Project (SISP), was unsuccessful, in part because so many bees died in captivity, in part because the insects proved more reliable at finding sugar water than bombs, in part because most soldiers would rather go into battle carrying an M16 than a box of bees.[21]

Other initiatives were more practical: researchers developed new machines to jam electronic signals from cell phones and other wireless devices with which insurgents triggered IEDs. Thousands of backpack-sized remote jammers were issued for patrols in IED country, foiling a number of attacks. Humvees were refitted with armor, while patrol vehicles were redesigned with a V-shaped undercarriage to deflect blasts. Robots were deployed to disable bombs. A simple piece of equipment known as the Rhino was developed—a ten-foot-long pole with a red-hot tip attached to the front of a truck, it set off IEDs in the vehicle's path, usually—but not always—rendering the bombs harmless. Blimps and drones were launched to keep an eye on bomb-planting insurgents. And troops were outfitted with more resilient body armor and helmets. These countermeasures undoubtedly saved lives, but deaths and injuries from IEDs continued as the Iraq War ended, the Afghanistan War ramped up, and determined enemies found new ways around the latest technical fix—a state of affairs that American military leaders see as a fixture of warfare for the foreseeable future.[22]

"We believe the use of IEDs will remain the most likely weapon of choice for violent extremist groups because they are low-cost, high-yield weapons that inflict maximum casualties at minimum risk and expense," said James Schear, deputy assistant secretary of defense for partnership strategy and stability operations.[23]

All the speeches and strategizing over IEDs were cold comfort for Jim and Alison Malachowski, who met their son's body at Dover Air Force Base in Delaware, viewed his remains there, and steeled themselves for a full-honors funeral at Arlington on April 7, 2011.[24]

The day of the service broke damp and cool, but the first signs of spring were showing at Arlington—ivory dogwoods in bloom, oaks fringed in a haze of pale green, tulips blooming orange and purple by the cemetery gates.[25]

Six body bearers from the Marine Corps Barracks in Washington met the silver hearse at McClellan Circle and transferred Staff Sergeant Malachowski's flag-covered casket to a caisson, watched over by comrades from a marching platoon, color guard, and firing party, all turned out in crisp blue coats and creased white trousers for the occasion. Members of the Marine Corps Band, ablaze in scarlet tunics and gold braid, raised their brass instruments, which caught the feeble sunlight as they launched into their version of the sturdy old hymn "Abide With Me." Body bearers snugged the Stars and Stripes tight over Malachowski's casket, tucked in the corners, and backed away from the caisson.[26]

A contingent from the Army's Old Guard, which provides horses, wagons, and riders for full-honors funerals, nudged six matched gray mounts into action, and the polished black caisson rattled down Marshall Drive in the direction of Section 60. Muffled drums and horses' hooves marked time. Mourners fell in behind. The procession—consisting of colors, band, marching platoon, caisson, body bearers, friends, and family—made a magnificent sight as it poured down through the green hills, hit the turn for York Drive, and swung right, where a line of dismounted motorcyclists from the Patriot Guard, many of them graying veterans of Vietnam in jeans and leather, stiffened and saluted just as the caisson creaked past them. It came to a stop. The funeral party caught up and stepped over the curb into Section 60, where the raw earth had been covered with green mats simulating grass. Out among the tombstones, the band struck up the Marine Hymn, a cue for the body bearers of Bravo Company ("We'll be the last to let you down") to slide their comrade's remains from the caisson and march his casket to the grave, stopping at last to lift him shoulder high, just as the last notes of the Marine Hymn faded.[27]

The Malachowski family filled the velvet-covered folding chairs in the front row, backed by friends and family clustering around them. A rabbi in civilian clothes officiated, reminding his audience that Marines had taken care of him when the bullets were flying in Da Nang, Kosovo, and Iraq. Now he was repaying the favor. "I'm here to extend condolences," he said, "and to . . . let you know that James's sacrifice was not in vain, that he has given his life for his country in the grandest and noblest cause. He was there to help us. If there is some consolation, it is in knowing that what he did was filled with pride and honor and dignity and courage."[28]

As the rabbi spoke, body bearers held the flag taut over Malachowski's casket, while his mother, father, and sister sat stiffly in their chairs, stunned by grief. At no point did they speak to or make contact with Lindsay Malachowski, Jimmy's widow, sitting beside them in the front row with Evan and Vincent, her two young boys by Jimmy.[29] War takes its toll on the best of marriages, and the Malachowskis, high school sweethearts who had endured four combat deployments and long separations, were no exception. Months before Jimmy's assignment in Afghanistan, the couple was living in different states and headed for divorce,[30] a rift that had still troubled Jimmy in the hours before his death. "Lindsay still hasn't sent me so much as a letter . . . sad face," he wrote in his last e-mail home from Afghanistan.[31]

At his graveside, the ritual of parting was winding down. The firing party let fly with three volleys; Taps floated over the cemetery; the band commenced the Navy Hymn, "Eternal Father, Strong to Save," which set the body bearers in motion. They slowly, lovingly, folded the flag into a blue triangle and passed it down the line to an officer who knelt before Lindsay Malachowski and presented it on behalf of the president of the United States and the commandant of the Marine Corps. He turned, took a second flag, and presented it to Alison as the rabbi offered a final prayer: "He who makes peace in the heavens grants peace to you in your distress, your discomfort, and your mourning . . . James, go in peace."[32]

At this, the mourners stood, filed by the casket for the last time, tossed handfuls of sand from a galvanized bucket, and placed sprays of roses on the casket for Jimmy. Marine Sgt. Danny Gonzalez stepped out of the crowd, unpeeled a red and yellow sticker, and stuck it to the casket's top. He knelt and kissed the sticker, which read, "U.S. Marine Corps Shooting Team," a reminder that Malachowski had not only been a highly skilled marksman but had also served as an instructor in combat marksmanship at Parris Island, South Carolina, where, between assignments in Iraq and Afghanistan, he had helped train more than fifty thousand recruits to shoot straight.[33]

Lindsay Malachowski, looking gaunt and isolated, huddled with her sons as the funeral party coalesced around Jimmy's parents and sister for final hugs. Gunnery Sgt. William J. Dixon, funeral director for Marine services at Arlington, slow-marched to the foot of Jimmy's grave, rendered a parting salute, slowly tugged off his white gloves, and laid them on the casket. With nothing left to say or do, the survivors drifted away, clearing the way for groundskeepers to see another Marine into the ground.[34]

★　★　★

Like many recent arrivals in Section 60, Malachowski had come home with catastrophic injuries, making it excruciating for his family to view his remains. His parents and sister did so with some trepidation, feeling it was the least they could do. For Alison, seeing her son in the mortuary at Dover Air Force Base was like seeing two people—perfectly normal from the waist up, horribly mangled from the waist down. Although the moment was traumatic for her, it became an important step in the grieving process.[35]

Other survivors with loved ones lost to the recent wars have been robbed of a final viewing, a ritual as old as warfare itself, because of the destructive impact of IEDs. If the fatal injuries are too disfiguring, casualty officers usually advise families against seeing the remains and recommend a closed casket for the traditional wake and funeral. Families have the final say in such matters, but in most cases they follow the advice of professionals.[36]

"These combatants come back horribly maimed—or they aren't all there," said Ami Neiberger-Miller, a public affairs specialist for the Tragedy Assistance Program for Survivors (TAPS), a nonprofit organization that has helped hundreds of grieving families cope with wartime losses. "Because IEDs cause catastrophic damage, seeing the remains is just too traumatic for most people." Neiberger-Miller gained firsthand experience on the subject when her own brother, Army Spec. Christopher T. Neiberger, twenty-two, was killed by a roadside bomb in Iraq in 2007. "The injuries were so bad that they advised against seeing Chris," she said. "So we never got to see my brother. It's something I understand but regret. It's characteristic of this war."[37]

Even survivors who view loved ones still face a long and often debilitating period of adjustment, which is perfectly normal but frightening for those going through the experience. "You think you're going crazy, like you're watching life from a great distance," said Darcie D. Sims, a psychologist who helps counsel families for TAPS. "If you're grieving, it's because you loved that person. Grief is the price we pay for love. This takes far longer than anybody expects. Each birthday is hard. The second year is harder than the first. Nobody expects that! You'll feel anger and guilt. You'll get depressed. We're surprised that the grieving is not finished—but that's because it will never be finished. But you can learn to manage it. And you don't have to do this alone. If you call TAPS, we will always answer 24/7. There are no answering machines in this family. We will walk through it with you as long as it takes."[38]

Weeks after her son's funeral, Alison Malachowski was still haunted by feelings that mothers have struggled with since the time of the Civil War: Had her son suffered in his last moments? Had he realized the severity of his injuries? Could he have survived? If he had survived, what would have been his quality of life?[39]

"All those things bothered me," she said. "He was conscious after the blast. I know that because he asked Sergeant Whorl if anyone else was hurt. That was Jimmy, worrying not about himself but his men. After he died, I felt this very strong urge to know exactly what happened. I felt that there was some force pushing me to find out, like Jimmy was pushing me to look into it."[40]

Although Alison and other family members had viewed Jimmy's remains upon his return to the United States, her compulsion over the circumstances of his death led her back to the time of his autopsy, as documented in photographs from his postmortem at Dover Air Force Base in Delaware. The images, on file at the Armed Forces Medical Examiner's Office in Rockville, Maryland, recorded the grisly details, which Alison reviewed with Army Maj. Dori Franco, a forensic pathologist from the medical examiner's office. Sitting side by side with

Franco in a conference room, Alison pored through the images and explicit diagrams for three hours. "Major Franco called up each picture, described to me what was in it, and asked if I was okay with seeing it," Alison recalled. "Then she showed it on her laptop. After a couple of hours she stopped and turned to me and said, 'I get it. I get it. You're supposed to find out.'" Alison viewed the images without her husband or daughter present. "They refused to go with me to Rockville. Enough already—they didn't want any part of it. But when I came out of that building and started driving home, I felt this tremendous burden lifted from me. It actually helped me come to terms with Jimmy's death. He was there with me, and all the way home I was crying and thanking him for making me do this."[41]

Reviewing her son's autopsy photographs convinced Alison that nothing could have been done to save him. Even if by some miracle he had survived, he almost certainly would have lost his legs, a fate he had feared worse than death. "I knew that because we talked about it, Marine to Marine, before he went to Afghanistan," said Alison. "Jimmy was a big, very physical guy. He ran six miles a day and pumped iron—if it was heavy, Jimmy would lift it. Before his last deployment, he grabbed me by the shoulders and told me that he'd rather die than come back missing limbs. I think he had some premonition of what was going to happen." She looked around Section 60, where several of her son's Arlington neighbors had expressed similar forebodings before leaving home for the last time.[42]

Alison was still mourning Jimmy's death in July 2011 when the surviving members of his much-diminished unit—Fox Company, Second Battalion, Eighth Marine Regiment—returned from Afghanistan to Camp Lejeune, in Jacksonville, North Carolina. "These guys were my new sons," said Alison, who drove down with her husband to welcome them home.[43]

The visit gave Jimmy's comrades an opportunity to reminisce about a respected leader and friend, which brought him briefly back to life and provided some degree of consolation for those present. "But the main reason we went to Lejeune," said Alison, "was to make it clear to Jimmy's guys that they had done everything to keep him alive. The building was cleared properly. Doc Deller [the medic] got right to him. They called the chopper quickly. Everybody did his job. Despite that, I know that some of them felt guilty about living. I know it's awkward for them to see me. What do you say to the dead guy's mother? I thought it would help if they heard from me that I didn't blame them, that there was nothing they could've done. I let Jimmy guide me in what I said to them." At Camp Lejeune, Alison tracked down her son's comrades and offered absolution; those she could not meet in person, she reached by e-mail with the same message: You did all you could.[44]

Despite such assurances, several Marines who served with Malachowski took his death hard, coming as it did on the heels of Ian Muller's killing a week before, and from a depressingly familiar source—a buried IED that had evaded detection. Lance Cpl. Matthew Westbrook, the dog handler who had seen Ian Muller blown to bits and who helped sweep the compound where Malachowski was killed, was sent home and medically retired because of memory loss, lurid nightmares, and headaches that made it impossible for him to continue working. Navy Corpsman Jesse "Doc" Deller, who vainly tried to save Muller and Malachowski, suffered from guilt as well as the stress of daily firefights at Patrol Base Dakota; he was transferred to a less volatile base in Helmand, where he completed his Afghan tour. Sgt. Tom Whorl, who had shared a room with Malachowski and served as his right-hand man, struggled with guilt and PTSD brewed by the brutalities he had witnessed again and again: carrying a fellow Marine's arm in a pack while others searched for the rest of his body, watching the life fade from a dying friend's eyes, packing a buddy's laptop and personal effects for shipment home, making calls to aggrieved families—all these things could grind down the most hardened combatant.[45]

"People always say don't feel guilty, that it was meant to be and shit like that. No, it is not," Whorl wrote a few weeks after the deaths of Malachowski and Ian Muller. "I have to write about this because it fills me with so much guilt, anger, sadness, and dread. Their deaths are the direct result of my decision, and I live with their faces in my mind every day, hear their voices . . . I live with my decisions every day and hate myself for them."[46]

Like others wrestling with the aftereffects of combat trauma, Whorl found it difficult to cross the threshold from war to peace. When he got home, he drank to deaden the pain, exploded in rages that frightened his children, jumped out of his skin at sudden noises, and squabbled with his wife, Nina, a Marine who had also served in Afghanistan. Awarded the Bronze Star for valor and promoted to staff sergeant upon his return home, Whorl now wore the chevrons he had unpinned from Malachowski's collar on the day of his death.

At Camp Lejeune, where Whorl reported for duty with the rest of his platoon, he tried to tough it out, followed the routines on base, and occasionally talked about his wartime experiences with buddies who had shared them. They understood. But he could not shake the guilt, anxiety, insomnia, and watchfulness that followed him home, or erase the memory of comrades dying that played in his mind over and over again. He spiraled into depression, cleaned out the medicine cabinet at home, and in November 2011 drove off into the night in his Pontiac G6, intent on killing himself. Hours later, after a frantic search, Nina found her husband barely conscious in his car at the Jacksonville Mall, bleeding from self-inflicted knife wounds to his arms and groggy from a massive overdose of the drugs meant to ease his transition from the battlefield.

She summoned an ambulance. He woke up in the intensive care unit of Onslow Memorial Hospital almost a week later with a breathing tube in his throat and his arms tied to the bedrails, confused about how he had landed there. Nina sat in a chair at his bedside, watching her husband slowly come back to life. With her prodding, he sought therapy for PTSD, entered the Wounded Warrior Regiment at Camp Lejeune, and realized that his life as a combat sergeant was over. He could no longer lead comrades into harm's way, knowing they would die.[47]

"Every time I think of the two I lost, I think of the forty-six I brought home, who have babies now, who have gotten married, who are doing great things with their lives," he told Brian Mockenhaupt, a writer who eloquently documented the experience of Whorl and others of the Second Battalion/ Eighth Marine Regiment.[48]

Two years after returning from Afghanistan, Whorl was medically discharged from the Marine Corps on disability, weeks before Nina also retired from service. Even now Whorl's sense of loss and sadness remains strong, but without the debilitating guilt that almost killed him. "The guilt isn't as bad as it was," he said recently, "but I still remember everything that happened to Ian and Jimmy—everything in detail. I still see them and hear them. I'm learning to manage it. A lot of therapy, really hard work. I had Nina behind me. If it wasn't for her, I would've been dead a long time ago."[49] The Whorls regularly make the rounds at Section 60, leaving coins and words of comfort for Jimmy Malachowski and other friends buried there.

It has been said that time heals all wounds, a maxim that prompts a derisive snort from Alison Malachowski. "It does not!" she said, sitting before the grave of her son two years after his death, the surrounding tableau of white tombstones and blue sky reflected in her sunglasses. "It doesn't get better. It just gets different. Some days I wake up, and for the first few minutes everything's

"It doesn't get better," said Alison Malachowski, a retired Marine sergeant, at the grave of her son, Staff Sgt. Jimmy Malachowski. (Robert M. Poole)

okay. Then I remember my son is dead, and everything crashes. People are nice. They try to be sympathetic, but unless you've gone through this, there's no way to understand." The tears flowed, she apologized, grabbed a tissue, and poked fun at herself. "God, where did that come from? Who is this crazy lady?" She laughed, hugged her knees, and cried some more.[50]

Section 60 is one of the few places in America where such outbursts are not only common but expected, where it is considered normal to speak to the dead. Here a perfect stranger may step from among the tombstones to offer a bear hug, a shot of whiskey, or a war story. This corner of Arlington is a safe zone where the grieving come to comfort one another, form new friendships, acknowledge love for those lost in wartime, and try to live with the wounds that persist long after the guns have fallen silent.

For Alison Malachowski and those who have suffered losses from the recent wars, Section 60 remains a sanctuary for private ritual, intense pride, and occasional solace. It is her last tangible point of contact with Jimmy, whom she visits on the twentieth of each month to mark the day he died. She comes to keep his memory alive, the smart, outdoorsy Maryland boy who collected butterflies and bugs, hung them in frames at home, won science prizes, read voraciously, loved classical music, and joined the Marines the day after graduating from high school. She often sits alone at his tombstone, which she decorates with so many fresh flowers, Mardi Gras beads, balloons, cigars, and toys that it is sometimes difficult to make out the name behind the mementos on his grave.[51]

On a recent morning between funerals, a damp wind rattled up from the Potomac and sent one of Jimmy's red-white-and-blue pinwheels spinning madly as Alison flourished a purple bag, tugged out a bottle of Crown Royal, and launched a toast for her son. A passerby joined her, as did a couple of Marines who had been visiting the grave of a friend. They strode over and happily joined Alison's salute. They talked about other Marines, the travails of this platoon or that battalion, and parted with hugs. Until something more permanent is established, Section 60 will function as memorial to the recent wars, a magnet for combatants and for families who want to remember those who are gone, and for citizens to see that the war goes on at Arlington, which continues adding graves.[52]

For most of a decade, Arlington's administrators have given a wide berth to grieving families whose grave decorations

Friends and families lavish decorations on the graves of Section 60.
(Robert M. Poole)

flagrantly violate the regulations banning all but the most minimal embellishments in Section 60. The Department of the Army, which has run Arlington since it was established as a national cemetery in Civil War days, allows visitors to decorate tombstones with fresh flowers in season and artificial ones in winter, with no provision for the idiosyncratic and sometimes exuberant mementos of recent years.

Much like the Vietnam War Memorial in Washington, Section 60 serves as a historical archive, where family and friends leave all kinds of material to document some aspect of the conflicts in Iraq and Afghanistan. They also bring personal gifts throughout the year: rabbit ears for Easter and pumpkins for Halloween, birthday balloons and cakes, memory stones the size of softballs, cookies, live ammunition, baby announcements, love letters, Bronze Star citations, short stories, children's drawings, zombie chainsaw stickers, toy soldiers, and offerings of beer and whiskey. Many of the newer tombstones have photographs glued or taped to them.[53]

"It's sometimes a bit over the top," said Ami Neiberger-Miller of TAPS, who frequently brings small decorations to her brother's grave in Section 60, "but most of it is harmless and well intentioned. This is the only memorial we have."[54]

Like others with relatives sleeping in Section 60, Alison Malachowski was stunned, on her regular visit to Arlington in July 2013, to find her son's grave stripped of flowers, toys, and other mementoes.[55]

"It was devastating," she said. "There was no warning—no announcement or anything. It didn't look like Section 60! I had to pinch myself to make sure I was in the right place. The little Humvee on Jimmy's grave was gone. It had been there for months. The toy rubber duck his sister Brandy had bought at the Pentagon was gone. Dog tags and a Purple Heart a friend had left—all gone. Not just Jimmy's grave but the whole place stripped clean. It was a shock."[56]

The sweep came shortly after Arlington's long-serving executive director, Kathryn A. Condon, retired as the cemetery's top administrator in July. She was succeeded by Patrick K. Hallinan, who cracked down on the impromptu memorials, citing cemetery regulations designed to maintain Arlington's

Pilgrims to Section 60 have embraced the Jewish tradition of decorating tombstones with rocks, one for each visitor. (Robert M. Poole)

signature aesthetic of orderly tombstones marching through manicured green hills.[57]

"We're following the secretary of the army's guidance regarding Section 60," said Jennifer Lynch, a spokeswoman for the cemetery, suggesting that the cleanup was not a change in policy but an effort to enforce established standards.[58] "The fact is that Arlington National Cemetery is not the Vietnam War Memorial," she said, ignoring the fact that visitors had left thousands of memorial objects for the dead in Section 60 over the last decade with little interference from cemetery officials. "It is a functioning cemetery, and we must remain true to that mission."[59]

In truth, Arlington is more than that, which caused families to protest the shift in policy. They notified the news media and complained to members of Congress, which prompted Hallinan, the cemetery's new director, to call for a closed meeting with families in October 2013. At that time he apologized profusely for the heavy-handed sweep in Section 60, explained why the shift was needed, and offered a mild compromise: in the future, he said, families would be allowed to leave

A love note for one of the many Navy SEALs lost in the recent wars.
(Robert M. Poole)

Arlington's administrators no longer tolerate photographs of the dead, like those taped on Pfc. Justin Davis's grave. (Robert M. Poole)

small "handcrafted" objects on graves, but no bottles, ammunition, or large stones, which could interfere with mowing. Any alcohol, tobacco, or other items he termed hazardous would be swept away. Survivors were welcome to place small pictures of loved ones by graves but could no longer affix such images to tombstones, which he characterized as a defacement of government property.[60]

Months after Hallinan's meeting with families, the controversy was still brewing. Some grieving families, who felt that they were being treated as criminals, continued to hang wind chimes and Christmas ornaments from trees in Section 60, while others doggedly offered alcoholic toasts to the dead. "What are they going to do to us—send us to jail for having a beer with a dead brother?" one asked recently.[61] For many families, the new policy was just one more disappointment on top of all the others. "It's heartbreaking," said Paula Davis, who lost her only son, Army Pfc. Justin Ray Davis, nineteen, to friendly fire in Afghanistan's Korengal Province in 2006.

For months after his death, she slept in his bed, hung his baby shoes on the doorknob of his room, and faithfully came to visit his grave in Section 60. You could set your watch by her arrival, always on Sunday, just after church. She tended his grave like a private garden, snipping the grass with scissors, setting out fresh flowers every week, and taping laminated photographs to his tombstone, where his smile beamed out for everyone to see. "Justin had the most beautiful smile," said his mother, who unintentionally showed where he got it. "That's what I want people to see . . . so he's not just a name and number of a tombstone. He's a person. That's what they're taking away."[62]

6

FRIENDLY FIRE

N O MATTER HOW often David Sharrett visits Section 60, he always feels the same sense of dislocation when he makes his way to Grave No. 60-8729, about halfway across the turf, and finds his name on a marble headstone. "It's like visiting my own grave," he said, standing before the tomb of Pfc. David H. Sharrett II, his namesake and first son, killed in Iraq in 2008. "Children are supposed to bury their parents, not the other way around."[1]

Private Sharrett's path to Arlington National Cemetery, and his father's quest to unravel the tangled story that brought his son there, hold enough plot twists for a Shakespearian tragedy—a fitting analogy, given that the elder Sharrett spent a distinguished thirty-year career teaching the Bard to several generations of high school students in northern Virginia.

Sharrett was just wrapping up a lesson on *Othello* when an otherwise ordinary morning—January 16, 2008—took a sinister turn, plunging him into the worst day of his life. Summoned to the office at Chantilly High School, he found James Charm, a family friend, waiting for him and looking very grim indeed.[2]

"Hey, what's up?" Sharrett asked.

"Vicki needs you to come," Charm said softly, referring to Sharrett's wife. "Vicki needs you to come home right away."

"What's wrong? Is it Dave?"

Charm did not—probably could not—answer.

"Is he okay?" Sharrett asked, panic rising.

"No," said Charm.

"Is he alive?"

Charm sadly shook his head from side to side.[3]

"Oh God, Oh God!" Sharrett sputtered, crying for the boy he had raised as a single father before Vicki came along. Father and son had been constant companions and best friends, joined at the hip, in Dave Senior's phrase. Young Dave, who bore a striking resemblance to his father, had accompanied him to school so often that the older students adopted him as a kind of mascot, nicknaming him "Bean" for his diminutive appearance.

He grew into an outgoing, fearless young man who loved life, made friends easily, and won statewide honors as a

Pfc. David H. Sharrett II, with his father, before going off to war.
(Sharrett family photo)

defensive end on the high school football team. After graduating in 1999, he knocked around at loose ends until 2006, when he joined the Army at age twenty-six. He soon qualified as a "Screaming Eagle" in the Army's elite 101st Airborne Division and found his way to Iraq. There he joined more than twenty thousand allied warriors flooding into the country as the surge of troops began in 2007.[4]

The soldiers in Sharrett's unit—Team Six of C Troop, First Squadron, 32nd Cavalry Regiment, First Brigade Combat Team—were fatefully pressed into action for Operation Hood Harvest, an Army offensive designed to weed out, chase down, and kill or capture insurgents thought to be affiliated with Al Qaeda. The enemy fighters, operating out of the Bichigan region, north of Baghdad, had been recruiting suicide bombers and harassing residents for weeks. To put a stop to their capers, the entire First Brigade Combat Team swept into Bichigan just before five A.M. on January 16, meeting no resistance. But six suspects fled the town before them, tracked by a network of helicopters and a surveillance drone. Sharrett's eight-man group, Team Six, clambered onto Black Hawk choppers and rushed to intercept the fleeing men, known in military jargon as "squirters" because they squeezed through the net that allies had set for them. Thought to be unarmed, the squirters scuttled out of Bichigan and into the frigid night, which was unlit by moon or stars. They hurried through a palm grove and crossed surrounding fields in single file, military style, before disappearing into a scrub thicket at the end of an irrigation ditch. There they took cover. Unbeknownst to the American troopers, the insurgents had cached weapons and ammunition in the thicket and were luring their pursuers into a trap.[5]

Sharrett's team, geared up and ready to fight, landed nearby and hit the ground running. Still believing the insurgents to be unarmed, the Americans approached the thicket with a decided lack of caution, closely surrounded their quarry, and shouted in English for them to come out.

"Allahu akbar!" one of the insurgents answered, emphasizing his response with a barrage of AK-47 fire and exploding hand grenades at close range, which sparked a nocturnal firefight. The thicket erupted in flames, jets and choppers swept in, and the countryside lit up for most of an hour. By the time it was over, all six insurgents had been killed, as well as two American troopers, Cpl. John P. Sigsbee and Pfc. Danny L. Kimme. Three other Americans lay wounded, including Sharrett, who bled to death before he could get to a military hospital. He became the 3,925th service member to die in Iraq.[6]

After families in the United States were notified of their sons' deaths, the Department of Defense cranked out the sort of press release that was becoming all too routine, a barebones summary of the action and its cost in American lives. Sharrett and two other troopers had been killed, the Pentagon announced, while "supporting Operation Iraqi Freedom . . . of wounds suffered . . . when they were attacked by grenade and small arms fire during combat operations."[7]

It was essentially this message—and very little else—that Master Sgt. James Blake, an Army casualty officer assigned to the Sharretts, relayed to family members on the day of his death, based on a very brief AR 15-6 report, an initial investigation of Private Sharrett's killing, which was assumed to be from enemy fire. "He had a large manila envelope," said Sharrett Senior, referring to Blake. "There were official documents he produced, but nothing that provided a glimpse into how Dave had been killed."[8]

Weeks, months, and years would pass before Sharrett's family pieced together the full story of their son's death, in part because of the chaotic nature of the firefight that claimed his life, in part because of secrecy surrounding the Army's investigation of its own actions, in part because Private Sharrett had, in truth, been killed by friendly fire, an embarrassment that officers were hesitant to elucidate. It did not help that Sharrett had died at a time when the Army was still reeling from the fratricide of Cpl. Pat Tillman, the pro football player turned solider accidentally shot by comrades in Afghanistan in 2004.[9] In that case, the Army destroyed crucial evidence, deceived family members, and blatantly misrepresented the facts surrounding Tillman's killing. Only after his family, the press, and congressional investigators demanded a full accounting did the Army fix responsibility for the death of its most famous soldier.[10]

The first inkling that the Army's initial account of Sharrett's death was grievously flawed came two days after his killing, when his remains arrived at Dover Air Force Base. According to protocol established early in the Afghanistan conflict, Sharrett was carefully examined by pathologists from the Armed Forces Medical Examiner's Office, who traced the trajectory of the fatal bullet that entered Sharrett's left buttock, ripped through his colon, mangled his prostate gland, and nicked his right femoral artery and vein before coming to rest in the soft tissue of his thigh; fragments of the bullet jacket were also found in his peritoneal cavity. The projectile was unmistakable, a copper-jacketed green-tipped 5.56-millimeter round made in America and issued to American forces in Iraq. Its presence in Sharrett's leg left no doubt that he had been shot by a comrade. Medical examiners ruled his death a homicide—although almost certainly an accidental one—and notified Sharrett's commanders in Iraq. They also sent word to Master Sgt. James Blake, the family's casualty officer in Virginia. Their findings triggered a second AR 15-6 investigation to establish who had fired the bullet.[11]

To update the family, Blake dutifully called the Sharretts and arranged a face-to-face meeting at their home in Oakton,

Virginia, on January 25, four days before the soldier's scheduled funeral at Arlington. Instead of forthrightly reporting the medical examiner's finding and informing the family of a new AR 15-6 investigation, Blake deepened the mystery by saying that Private Sharrett had *possibly* died from friendly fire.[12]

"Oh shit," said Sharrett's stepmother, Vicki. "You mean this is like Pat Tillman?"[13]

"At least he wasn't killed by some scumbag terrorist," the elder Sharrett blurted, later admitting that he had said something stupid in the emotional turbulence of the moment. Inconclusive as it was, Blake's news hit hard. Vicki broke down in tears. Sharrett brooded over the indignity of fratricide. "Friendly fire had become a stigma to me," Sharrett said, "something I was beginning to perceive as untoward—and beneath Dave. He was too tough, too smart, to have put himself in that kind of compromising position, and it didn't sit right with me." He recalled one of his son's last letters, jarringly ironic in hindsight: "Don't worry about me," Dave had written, trying to reassure his father, "I won't let some fucking Arab kill me."

Still reeling from Blake's latest news, Sharrett asked if one of his son's commanders could provide more detail about the firefight. Blake agreed to try, expressed his condolences again, and left the Sharretts struggling to absorb the latest shock. Back at his office near Washington, D.C., Blake arranged for Lt. Col. Robert H. McCarthy III, the squadron commander for Operation Hood Harvest, to call the Sharretts.

A few hours later McCarthy was on the line from Iraq. "I was your son's battalion commander," McCarthy announced over the crackle and static of the long-distance connection. "First, let me express my deep condolences for your son's death, Mr. Sharrett."

"Thank you for calling, sir," Sharrett said. "This is a very hard time for us. We don't know anything about what happened to Dave on January sixteenth, and the Army hasn't given us any details. Can you tell me about it?"

McCarthy launched into a detailed description of the firefight, the terrain, the fleeing suspects, and the particulars, but with so many acronyms and so much specialized language that Sharrett soon lost the thread—a classic case, he admitted later, of a Shakespeare teacher and an Army colonel speaking different languages. Sharrett, sitting at the kitchen table, listened until the end of McCarthy's narrative, which had said nothing about friendly fire.

"Colonel McCarthy," Sharrett said, "our casualty assistance officer came to our home and informed us that Dave was killed by friendly fire."

"That is *not* true!" McCarthy shouted down the line, so loud that Vicki, who was hovering nearby, heard him across the room. Coming a few hours after the message that Private Sharrett had been a victim of fratricide, McCarthy's emphatic denial whipsawed the family off course. Now they were back to the original narrative, believing that their son had been shot by an enemy. Reassured by McCarthy's version of events, Sharrett thanked the colonel and asked for a letter summarizing their discussion. McCarthy obliged with a lengthy e-mail, which the Sharretts received two days later.[14]

McCarthy sketched out the larger goals of Operation Hood Harvest, which was "to clear the village of Bichigan (population of approximately 3,000 people) of terrorists and clear the surrounding orchards of potential weapons caches." He continued:

The purpose was to deny terrorist influence over the local population and establish a Concerned Local Citizen's Group (a local force to secure the village, akin to an armed neighborhood watch). Al Qaeda was reportedly using the area as a sanctuary and was intimidating the local population into supporting them . . . In the early morning (pre-dawn), aircraft supporting the operation observed six individuals running from a palm grove. No weapons were observed. Dave's element landed and moved toward the fleeing men. As the helicopters approached this group of men, they hid in a thicket of dense vegetation in an irrigation ditch.

Dave's element surrounded the brush and conducted a verbal "call-out" in an attempt to get them to surrender. As Dave's element surrounded the position, the enemy opened fire at very close range, touching off a fierce grenade and small arms fight that resulted in the deaths of Dave, CPL John Sigsbee, and PFC Danny Kimme . . . All six enemy fighters were killed . . . On 24 Jan 08, the Sheik controlling the Bichigan area detained 6 more terrorists, to include both the primary target of our operation the morning David was killed . . . and delivered them to control of the Iraqi Police. They have now decided to take control of their area and reject the presence of terrorists in their midst. Their fight is far from over, but they appear to have now chosen sides and they appear to have chosen to take a stand against terrorism. David and his team's efforts played a key role in emboldening them to make that choice. Fathers in Bichigan can now hope to put their children in bed at night, without fearing that strange men will bang on their door . . . demand food and lodging, and potentially harm or kill them.

McCarthy's note was obviously well intended, meant to show that Private Sharrett had died in a noble cause. But the e-mail also reinforced the impression that Sharrett had been shot by an enemy—not by one of his own comrades. Although as squadron commander McCarthy knew of Sharrett's fratricide within hours of the firefight, nowhere in his 574-word e-mail did he mention friendly fire. When investigators quizzed him about this omission in a follow-up probe, McCarthy offered several reasons: he thought the Sharretts already knew their son had died from friendly fire; he refrained from mentioning fratricide because he thought the elder Sharrett might use language from his January 27 e-mail for his son's eulogy; he knew the Army had mounted a new AR 15-6 investigation focused on friendly fire but wanted to wait for the results before sharing details with Sharrett's family.[15]

Whatever his reason for withholding details, McCarthy had plenty of company in his gingerly approach to fratricide. "There is a powerful bias against officially reporting fratricide in war," said Kenneth K. Steinwig, writing in *Parameters*, the quarterly journal of the U.S. Army War College. "It is such a sensitive topic that few people have attempted to study it, and until very recently, no one has systematically looked at the issue. The assumption that fratricide is a rare event reinforced these biases."[16]

In reality, fratricide has a long kinship with armed conflict, reaching back to the War of the Roses in fifteenth-century England. In that instance, when King Edward IV clashed with the Earl of Warwick in 1471, Warwick's men fatefully misidentified a key ally in the fog, rained arrows on his position, and lost the Battle of Barnet, which ended with Warwick's head on a platter.[17]

Closer to home, then-Col. George Washington, commanding a British regiment of five hundred Virginians in the French and Indian War in November 1758, encountered a contingent of fellow Virginians at dusk near Fort Ligonier, Pennsylvania. Each regiment mistook the other for French enemies. Musket balls flew in all directions, claiming forty friendly casualties. Washington, caught between the lines, wrote later that the skirmish was the closest call he ever had.[18]

Because friendly fire has likely been underreported, it is difficult to gauge its toll in past conflicts. The most conservative estimate, from the Army's Aeromedical Research Laboratory in Fort Rucker, Alabama, suggests that fratricide was responsible for 14 percent of U.S. troops wounded in World War I; 12 to 16 percent of those killed or wounded in World War II; 7 percent killed or wounded in Korea; and 11 to 14 percent killed or wounded in Vietnam. With the advent of Desert Storm, also known as the Persian Gulf War, the numbers spiked, with friendly fire accounting for 15 percent of those wounded and 24 percent of those killed. This alarming jump in casualties prompted the armed forces to emphasize preventive training and to keep better records.[19] For reasons that are still uncertain, the number of those killed or wounded by friendly fire reached unprecedented levels in the Iraq War, where fratricide accounted for as much as 40 percent of all casualties, according to the writer Jon Krakauer; in Afghanistan, the rate, at 13 percent and falling as operations wind down, was more consistent with historic levels.[20]

Still believing that their son had died trading shots with the enemy, the Sharretts converged on Arlington National Cemetery for his funeral on January 29, 2008. The day of the service was cold and damp, ushered in by a late-night thunderstorm rumbling offstage. A long line of cars, led by a silver hearse, rolled up the wet streets to the cemetery gates on Memorial Drive. "I looked out the window at a massive line of idling cars and thought, *There must be another funeral going on*," Sharrett said. "But as I began to recognize the faces . . . I realized they were all there for Dave and for me and for our family." The procession made its way along Eisenhower Drive and down through the aisle of trees to Section 60, where the family—including Private Sharrett's widow, Heather Shine, his birth mother, and his two surviving brothers—emerged from their cars and headed for a roped-off plot among the tombstones. "We were escorted to a row of chairs on a green, oversized mat of artificial turf laid over the sloshy mud and positioned in front of Dave's casket," Sharrett said. "I sat there transfixed with a sight I'd always feared—a military chaplain went through a short liturgy and prayed for us all."[21]

The ceremony ran its familiar course, imposing the impression of order on the uncertainty of the moment. A firing party from the Old Guard shouldered their weapons and punched out a three-rifle volley; Taps rang on the chill air; a two-star general knelt to present the Purple Heart and Bronze Star medal to the dead soldier's survivors; multiple flags were folded tight and tendered to those on the front row; and David H. Sharrett II was committed to the earth.[22]

One of the dignitaries present that day was Sen. John W. Warner of Virginia, himself a combat veteran, then serving as chairman of the Senate Armed Services Committee. He huddled with another official mourner, Rep. Frank Wolf of Virginia, and was overheard saying, "You know, they're investigating this as friendly fire." This offhand comment, delivered at graveside and relayed to Sharrett later that day, undercut the message that Colonel McCarthy had conveyed just two days before. What was it, friendly fire or enemy action? Sharrett, off-balance and confused, was insulted by Warner's remark. "On the day we buried Dave, they knew more than I did about his dismal fate," he said.[23] "I needed information. I was completely clueless."[24]

Private Sharrett, though buried, was hardly at rest. Like the ghost of Hamlet's father, the young soldier continued to haunt family members and comrades struggling to make sense of his killing. In this modern drama, however, the roles were reversed, with the son visiting his father in the wee hours. The dream was always the same: Sharrett Senior goes to the airport to welcome his son home. The soldier strides down the ramp, which is surrounded by a sea of well-wishers greeting other returning warriors. But something is wrong. "Dave lingers behind," said Sharrett. "We see each other, start talking, and he says to me, 'I can't come with you, Pop.' I say, 'I know,' and he fades into a blur. I wake up crying."[25]

While Sharrett wrestled with this nightmare, forensic investigators were busy analyzing the bullet that had killed his son. They compared signature markings on the fatal round with those from rifles the troopers had carried into the firefight on January 16. An exact match was made on February 20, 2008, showing that the bullet had been fired by Lt. Timothy R. Hanson, the senior officer who led Team Six into the fight at Bichigan.[26] He continued to command troops as the investigation ran its course.[27]

The ballistics evidence was folded into the Army's second AR 15-6 report, which was approved by Maj. Gen. Mark Hertling, commander of the Army's First Armored Division, on February 22, 2008. Then, for reasons that are still unclear, the report languished in the coils and recesses of the bureaucracy for three months before it was presented to Sharrett's family on May 29.[28]

This was the first time they learned unequivocally that Private Sharrett had been killed by friendly fire. The news was delivered by Master Sgt. James Blake, the family's casualty officer, who had last seen the Sharretts at their son's funeral. In the months since that bleak January day, the elder Sharrett had retired from teaching and moved with his family to Forest, Virginia, three hours away in the foothills of the Blue Ridge Mountains.[29]

Brushed and polished in his dress blues for the occasion, Blake revealed new findings documenting the fratricide and showing how Operation Hood Harvest had turned disastrous. First, the thick report said, the number of men in Sharrett's troop—eight soldiers in all—had been too few to go after six enemy suspects; the usual rule of thumb is a force ratio of three to one. Second, members of Lieutenant Hanson's Team Six had incautiously approached the thicket and surrounded it, in effect forming a circular firing squad; this increased the chances of fratricide when the shooting started. Third, in their rush to intercept the insurgents, five of the eight soldiers on Team Six had failed to activate their "bud lights," small battery-powered strobes visible only to allies equipped with night vision goggles. The infrared lights, which combatants usually carry in a thigh pocket of their cargo pants, help soldiers distinguish friend from foe in nighttime combat. Hanson and Staff Sgt. Chris "Coach" McGraw, the team's ranking noncommissioned officer, were faulted for letting their men go into battle without activating the markers; so were the five soldiers who failed to do so, which contributed to the death of Sharrett, according to the report. Finally, the document noted that Hanson, after accidentally shooting Sharrett, had left the action and boarded a chopper at 6:10 A.M. with two wounded comrades; he had not located three dead and wounded soldiers still on the battlefield and provided no guidance for other soldiers, who then began a frantic search for Sharrett and other casualties.[30]

When Blake reached this part of the AR 15-6 report, his eyes widened, according to Sharrett Senior, sitting across from him at the kitchen table. "Man, there's something wrong here. Never ever would anybody do that," Blake said, referring to Hanson's early departure from battle.

"Dave was out there dying and this guy just cut and ran?" Sharrett blurted.

"Affirmative, Mr. Sharrett," Blake said, shaking his head.[31]

When Hanson exited the fight, he was unwounded. He said later that he left to take care of two badly injured teammates, Staff Sergeant McGraw and Spec. Raphael Collins.[32] However, they testified that he had done nothing to administer aid while in transit, nothing to help them off the chopper at the hospital, and nothing to find medics to treat them when they stumbled into the hospital and had to search for help. Hanson remained on the bird, which then returned to Forward Operating Base Paliwoda in Balad for refueling.[33] There Hanson disembarked, went to his barracks, and broke down, sobbing. "I think there is a possibility we may have killed somebody out there," he told an officer who came to check on him shortly after the firefight. Nobody asked what he meant by "we" or "somebody."[34] Nor did he say why he had left dead and wounded soldiers behind, a clear violation of the Warrior Ethos. Maj. Rob Young, the investigator who prepared the new AR 15-6 report, gently criticized Hanson and other leaders for poorly planning and executing the mission, but he recommended no punishment. "I did not find any violations of the law, regulations, or policies during this investigation," Young wrote.[35]

Sharrett Senior was struck by how amateurish the operation had been. Why had Hanson's team assumed that it was safe to approach the thicket, even if the six insurgents were reported to be unarmed? The suspects were Al Qaeda affiliates—no less an authority than Colonel McCarthy had said so. Why had the Americans sent eight of their soldiers up against six of the enemy? And who had ordered the Americans to rush the thicket?

When Sharrett posed these questions to McCarthy, the ranking officer for Operation Hood Harvest, he was rebuffed. "The answers to your questions would be drawn from the Rules of Engagement and sensitive intelligence reporting, both of which are classified Secret," McCarthy e-mailed him. "Your Casualty Assistance Officer can assist you in submitting a Freedom of Information Act request for this information. I am not very confident it will be declassified." Sharrett got the same cool treatment when he queried McCarthy about Hanson's performance at Bichigan.

It was soon clear that Hanson had crumpled in the heat of combat, his first experience in battle. "Hanson went into a meltdown—he just lost it," his regimental commander admitted to the elder Sharrett.[36] "He was scared as hell," one of Hanson's soldiers said, recalling how the leader of Team Six had scrambled to safety as a fresh relay of troopers, from a dismounted reconnaissance unit designated Team Four, arrived to shore up the mission.[37] One of these troopers, Spec. Jurwien Fuentes, recalled Hanson's panicked exit. "His exact words still make me so angry," said Fuentes. "We're getting shot at and I don't know where my guys are," Hanson had said, dashing toward the chopper.[38]

As Hanson flew away, Fuentes and other members of Team Four moved on the thicket, silenced the last sputters of enemy fire, and desperately began searching for dead and wounded comrades. Because Hanson had provided no clue as to where his men had fallen, it took almost twenty precious minutes for Fuentes and company to locate Sharrett. By some miracle he was still alive, with a faint pulse, when they found him at about 6:30 A.M. Sharrett's rescuers summoned a medevac chopper, which took another ten minutes to arrive on the scene. Sharrett was finally evacuated at 6:50 A.M., ninety minutes after being shot. He was dead on arrival at the hospital in Balad.[39]

There the team leader, Staff Sergeant McGraw, whose arm had been badly mangled by an enemy grenade, caught a last glimpse of Sharrett, lying on a hospital table. Medics worked over the soldier's limp form, frenetically pumping his chest. "Don't quit!" McGraw yelled at them. "Wake the fuck up!" he shouted at Sharrett, who was beyond hearing. His tour of Iraq was over.[40]

Reassigned to a desk job for the remainder of his deployment, Hanson provided two sworn statements about the firefight, admitting in neither that he had killed Sharrett.[41] Although the second AR 15-6 investigation erroneously concluded that

Hanson had mistaken Sharrett for "an enemy fleeing the thicket," video footage of the incident, filmed by Apache helicopters and other aerial sources, showed otherwise. In the video, Private Sharrett ran away from the thicket to seek cover on the same line that Hanson had taken. He was six feet to Hanson's left when the lieutenant shot him. In order to do that, Hanson had to swing and fire his weapon at a 45-degree angle, away from the insurgents' hiding place.

Confronted with the video three years after the event, Hanson could not explain why he had shot Sharrett—he had fired blindly at brush where he thought the insurgents were holed up. "Well, I—it was—I mean it was pitch black, sir. It was kind of disorienting," Hanson told an Army officer detailed to document the incident.[42]

Hanson's account was peppered with such inconsistencies. He testified that he heard the insurgents talking from their cover almost fifty feet away—yet he did not hear the 210-pound, six-foot-tall Sharrett fall mortally wounded, in full body armor, six feet away from him. Hanson said Sharrett never cried out.

"You never heard anything?" the investigator asked, incredulous. "You could hear the voices from the insurgents possibly ten or fifteen meters away but you couldn't hear a sound after someone hit the ground or . . ."

"No sir," Hanson stammered. "I, I fired and took off."[43]

As evidence of Hanson's performance mounted, the elder Sharrett pressed for punishment. He was joined in this request by Doug Kimme, the father of Pfc. Danny Kimme, one of the two soldiers killed by enemy fire at Bichigan. Sharrett and Kimme appealed to Col. Michael S. McBride, Hanson's brigade commander in Iraq. Largely to placate the aggrieved fathers, McBride wrote a blistering letter of reprimand, taking Hanson to task for "failing to exercise adequate command and control over your platoon on 16 January, 2008.[44] Specifically," McBride continued,

You are being reprimanded for your failure to conduct movement and actions on contact rehearsals prior to the operation, identify and emplace a support by fire element with overwatch of the enemy position, and maintain communication with the Soldiers under your command. Your conduct contributed directly to the death of one of your Soldiers from friendly fire.

As a leader, you are expected to possess the tactical competency necessary to achieve mission success. Your conduct demonstrates a marked lack of proficiency in basic platoon leader skills. Instead of minimizing the risk to your Soldiers, you compounded it. Your mission was ill-planned and poorly executed, resulting in grievous consequences to the unit.

Based on your actions, I have grave doubts concerning your potential for future military service . . . I am considering whether to recommend . . . that this memorandum be filed in your Official Military Personnel File. Before deciding whether to forward this memorandum for a filing determination, I will consider the recommendations of your chain of command as well as any matters you wish to submit.[45]

The letter proved to be a slap on the wrist, more for show than substance. In Army parlance, it was placed in Hanson's "local" file. This meant that nobody saw it after the lieutenant completed his sixteen-month tour of Iraq and returned to Fort Campbell, Kentucky, late in the autumn of 2008. By then the reprimand had been shredded, so that the Army had no permanent record of Hanson's performance at Bichigan. He remained in the service, transferring to a reserve-training unit in his native Wisconsin. An Army promotion board, ignorant of Hanson's "local" reprimand, promoted him to captain in March 2009.[46] He even earned the prestigious Combat

Infantryman Badge—a silver Springfield rifle on a sky blue field—which tells the world that a soldier has "satisfactorily performed" his duties "in active ground combat, to close with and destroy the enemy with direct fire." The action for which Hanson received the badge occurred on January 16, 2008— the day he killed Sharrett.[47]

The elder Sharrett was aghast. "What in the world is this guy doing leading men into battle? Why was this guy in charge of my son?" he asked.[48] "I couldn't believe they were protecting Hanson."[49] Under prodding from Sharrett, McBride belatedly came to the conclusion that Hanson had no business in the Army. In the spring of 2009—thirteen months after the friendly fire incident—McBride moved to make Hanson's temporary reprimand a permanent part of his official file, a move that would end any soldier's career. "It is MY mission to see this through," McBride assured Sharrett Senior. The colonel forwarded his recommendation to commanders of the 101st Airborne Division.[50]

In a surprise twist, McBride was overruled by Brig. Gen. Steven J. Townsend, deputy commander of the 101st Airborne, who concluded that Hanson had suffered enough. Hanson, Townsend said, was "living every day with the heavy burden that his personal mistakes contributed to the deaths of his men and directly caused the death of PFC Sharrett." Citing reviews by unnamed commanders, Townsend determined that Hanson should receive no punishment. The soldier had learned from his hard experience and "continued to serve well since this incident and was recently promoted to Captain by the Army. Allegations that the unit or the Army withheld or concealed information from the families are completely baseless."[51]

Townsend and other senior officers, closing ranks around Hanson, were increasingly annoyed with Sharrett. "Mr. Sharrett will not be satisfied no matter what we do," General

Townsend complained to superiors. Townsend's Pentagon bosses also heard from Kelly Tyler, Fort Campbell's spokeswoman, who suggested that Sharrett's concerns should take a back seat to the Army's larger interests: "We may rapidly be approaching the point where respecting and understanding Mr. Sharrett's grieving process becomes secondary to defending the actions of the leadership involved in this incident," she wrote in an e-mail she mistakenly thought would be kept secret.[52]

At this juncture, Sharrett felt that Army leaders had abandoned Dave all over again. Veering between pity for Hanson and anger at the officers still shielding him, Sharrett considered giving up.[53] A devout Christian, he wanted to forgive the man who had killed Dave and get on with life. "This has devastated the guy," Sharrett told a friend. "I know that. I hurt for the guy. I didn't wish for his suffering."[54] But whenever he sank into pity for Hanson, Sharrett said, "that cold headstone in Section 60 spoke to me. Dave couldn't speak for himself. I had to give my son a voice. I always taught my students to do the right thing. Now I had to."[55]

Sharrett turned to one of those former students, James Gordon Meek, to chart a new battle plan.[56] Meek, a seasoned reporter working as a Washington correspondent and national security specialist for the *New York Daily News*, helped his old teacher negotiate the labyrinthine corridors of the Pentagon, unearth records through Freedom of Information requests, and uncover previously secret videos of the fatal firefight, which showed Private Sharrett writhing on the ground while Hanson scampered to safety. Fellow soldiers from Sharrett's old Army unit, disgusted by what they considered a cover-up by higher-ups, began feeding Sharrett, Meek, and Doug Kimme firsthand information from the firefight.

Meek's first article on the case, prominently displayed in the *Daily News* of April 1, 2009, broke through the wall of silence the Army had erected around Hanson and his superiors. "Army Lied About How My Son Died in Iraq," the headline on Meek's story thundered. "Army brass in Iraq whitewashed an incident of a soldier killed by his own lieutenant by blaming the dead hero, stonewalling his family and promoting his killer, the *Daily News* has learned." Meek's article set off tremors at the Pentagon and a new wave of media interest in the story, which would be covered by National Public Radio, *Army Times*, and the *Washington Post.*[57] Tom Jackman, the *Post* reporter who resolutely pursued Sharrett's story, even posted chilling videos of the Bichigan firefight on his paper's website.[58]

After crusading solo for so long, Sharrett was no longer alone. In December 2009 he wrote a heartfelt appeal to Gen. George W. Casey, Jr., the Army chief of staff, asking him to review the two previous investigations of his son's death and its aftermath. He pointed to the poor planning for Operation Hood Harvest and his struggle to wrest basic information about Dave's death out of the Army. He noted gaps and inconsistencies in previous investigations, one of which seemed to blame Dave for his own death. He asked that leaders responsible for the mishandling of the Bichigan raid be held accountable.[59]

Sharrett, a former college football star who sprinkles conversation with sports metaphors, conceded that professional soldiers might "argue that a civilian has no right playing Monday morning quarterback about a combat incident they were not a witness to. They would say that only combatants have the right to second-guess decisions made during a mission that went awry on a moonless night when bullets were flying. Maybe so. But," he continued,

> When the combatants investigate themselves like they're a junior varsity squad instead of like professionals, when they fumble notifying Gold Star families of the full truth, when

they grudgingly agree under outside pressure to hold one leader accountable in the most meaningless manner and then reverse a battlefield commander's ultimate judgment call, then those who gave up all they had . . . deserve a voice only their loved ones can provide. Sir, I proudly and unapologetically speak for Pfc. Sharrett.[60]

Moved by Sharrett's letter and the lively media interest in the case, Casey ordered a high-level review of the friendly fire incident and its aftermath early in 2010. Brig. Gen. David J. Bishop, an Iraq veteran and former armored battalion commander, was given the thankless job of reopening the case. He plowed through old reports and e-mails, pored over witness statements from the two earlier AR 15-6 probes, and scrutinized previously unseen tapes of the firefight that Private Sharrett's former teammates had turned up. In August 2010 Bishop invited Sharrett's family to the Pentagon to watch one of the new tapes with Lt. Gen. William Troy, director of the Army staff.

Crowding into a tiny room where the lights had been dimmed, Sharrett watched the action unfold on a big television screen, where he "watched my son die . . . He was sprawled out on an infrared terrain, his body heat casting him as a white silhouette on a gray field. My rage simmered as I watched him writhing in pain . . . and then the lieutenant limping to a Black Hawk while abandoning Dave and his buddies . . . Part of me was dying in the corner of the screen. I wondered what he thought about as it all slipped away. I hoped it was me."

When the film dissolved and the lights came up, one of Sharrett's sons, Chris, then twenty-one and an Air Force intelligence officer, stiffened, broke the silence, and addressed the senior officer in the room: "I just watched a man get left behind," Chris icily told General Troy. Troy stared back.

Bishop, looking uncomfortable, answered for all the others: "From a Warrior Ethos standpoint, he shouldn't have left," said Bishop, who then offered an excuse for Hanson: "He said he was helping the wounded."

"That's bullshit," David Sharrett blurted. "It's a lie."

Two years after Private Sharrett joined the ranks at Arlington, people were still arguing about what had happened at Bichigan. There was no clear, agreed-upon version of the event—and no punishment for Timothy Hanson, who was still commanding troops and drawing Army pay as 2011 unfolded. On the third anniversary of Sharrett's death, the Army, still under bombardment from Sharrett Senior and his allies, determined to take a final look at the controversy. Lt. Gen. William J. Troy, newly appointed as director of the Army staff, ordered a new AR 15-6 investigation—the third one undertaken by the Army. Once again General Bishop was tapped to head the probe, which was charged with clearing up allegations of a cover-up, inconsistencies in testimony by Hanson and other witnesses, and lapses in training and planning for Operation Hood Harvest.

Bishop, a thorough and fair-minded investigator, called many of the key characters back onto stage, reprising testimony from Hanson, Sharrett, and McCarthy. After weeks of probing, including travel to various Army bases, Bishop overturned key findings of earlier inquiries while confirming others: Hanson had not mistaken Sharrett for an enemy gunman but had been firing blindly when he accidentally cut down the young trooper; by crowding the insurgents and encircling them, Hanson's men had put themselves at risk from enemy fire and friendly fire; planning for Operation Hood Harvest had been adequate, but Hanson's failure to rehearse for the raid contributed to the mission's failure; McCarthy had not intentionally misled Sharrett Senior about his son's death. "I believe that a miscommunication occurred between [Colonel McCarthy]* and Mr. Sharrett," Bishop said. "I cannot resolve the source of that miscommunication due to the passage of time since the conversation took place over three years ago." Bishop absolved McCarthy and other superiors of any cover-up. Squadron leaders had begun investigating the possibility of fratricide within hours of the firefight.[61]

Bishop painstakingly cataloged Hanson's mistakes again. He had not met "the expectations of an officer of his grade and experience due to the failure to maneuver his unit and the adverse outcome of the engagement. He also failed to participate in movement and actions on contact rehearsals or ensure they were conducted. Finally, he accidentally shot one of his own Soldiers. He was issued a locally filed LOR (Letter of Reprimand) by his Brigade Commander, Col. McBride, as punishment for these failures." Bishop said that Hanson's reprimand had been no stronger for a simple reason: his superior officers felt sorry for him.[62] "The chain of command," he wrote,

> ... demonstrated compassionate deference to [Hanson] in their sworn statements, due to his participation in such an intense, long duration, close quarters small arms and grenade engagement and due to his having lost Soldiers under his leadership. I believe that the prevailing belief among the chain of command was to not question his character, but rather, to focus on the tactical efforts that triggered the situation in the first place ... [Hanson] went on to serve successfully in his assignment as Troop Executive Officer for the remainder of his 14 month OIF (Operation Iraqi Freedom) deployment ... Furthermore, there were extenuating

---

* Under the Army's privacy rules, the names of all living service members are redacted from reports made available to the public. In cases where the identity of the person mentioned is clear from the context, the author includes the name in brackets.

circumstances which further mitigated the circumstances to a degree. Taking further action after three years would be inappropriate.[63]

Bishop was less charitable about Hanson's behavior in the aftermath of battle, which he characterized as inexcusable—and an abdication of duty. By leaving the field prematurely, Hanson might have doomed Private Sharrett, who was still alive when his lieutenant flew to safety. "Had [Hanson] remained to assist with the search for [Sharrett and other soldiers unaccounted for,]" he wrote, "he may have looked in the vicinity of Pfc. Sharrett's original location by the bush. Another person looking in that area may have helped locate him sooner. This is only speculation, and there is no way of knowing if the additional 10–13 minutes would have made a difference in saving Pfc. Sharrett's life."[64]

Bishop believed that Hanson deserved a harsher penalty than the temporary letter of reprimand for his "inexplicable departure from the battlefield while four of his Soldiers were still unaccounted for and without conducting an adequate battle handover; for his failure to uphold the . . . Warrior Ethos; and for his lack of regard for completing his assigned mission and ensuring the welfare and safety of his Soldiers."[65]

Whether the Army followed through with Bishop's recommended penalty is unknown, because under personnel rules of the service, the proposed sanction was redacted from Bishop's report.[66] However, it is almost certain that Bishop proposed a permanent letter of reprimand because, soon after the brigadier's memorandum made its rounds, such a letter was signed by a general officer and placed in Hanson's permanent file, ending his career in uniform. This action, known as a General Officer Memorandum of Reprimand (GOMOR), triggered others, notably the stripping of Hanson's Combat

Infantryman's Badge on June 14, 2012, after a Senior Army Decorations Board voted unanimously to revoke it.[67]

Hanson quietly left the Army shortly after that, resolute in his refusal to speak about Sharrett's death.[68] The controversy stalled the career of Hanson's main defender, Lt. Col. Robert McCarthy, whose nomination to full colonel, which should have won routine approval in the Senate, died there in January 2013, bottled up in committee.[69]

"My son's voice was finally heard," said Sharrett Senior, who felt no particular joy—just a sense of relief and vindication—at Hanson's departure and the turmoil attending it. Armed only with his fierce love for his son, an English teacher had taken on the U.S. Army and won—finally a bit of good news he could share with Dave the next time he visited Section 60.[70]

7

THE LONG WAY HOME

MOST OF THE recent arrivals in Section 60 come from Iraq and Afghanistan, but they rest among warriors from earlier conflicts—from Vietnam, Korea, and even World War II. Every few months or so, one of these long-lost combatants is uncovered in some distant land, repatriated, identified by DNA or other evidence, and brought to Arlington for final honors.

In many cases the homecomings take place long after families of the dead have disappeared, but they still have brothers and sisters in uniform who remember who they were and what they did, even if the action that claimed them occurred fifty or sixty years before. In this part of the cemetery, the delay makes the ritual of parting all the more poignant when it finally takes place. The passing years also tend to soften the politics associated with past conflicts. The rightness of a particular war matters little here; what counts is that some young person suited up and did his duty, only to perish in a plane crash in a

Laotian jungle or a firefight on some obscure Pacific atoll or in a freezing prisoner-of-war camp on the Korean peninsula.

"Everybody who gets here earns the four-star treatment," said Army First Sgt. Robert A. Durbin, a member of the Old Guard who served tours in Iraq and Afghanistan and now oversees full-honors funerals for the Army's highly respected Honor Guard Company at Fort Myer. He led a visitor through Section 60 on a cool spring afternoon, walking among the graves of comrades killed in the recent wars, as well as those who would qualify for great-grandfather status today, had they lived out their lives.[1]

One such soldier, Army Cpl. A. V. Scott of Detroit, would be ninety-one years old now. He disappeared at age twenty-seven on February 12, 1951, when Chinese forces overran his unit, the 503rd Field Artillery Battalion of the Second Infantry Division, in the Korean War. Captured with scores of other American soldiers east of Seoul, he was marched a hundred miles to a POW camp in Huanghae Province of North Korea. Scott died there of exhaustion and dysentery in April of that year. Comrades committed him to a makeshift grave that would hold him for the next forty years, through the cease-fire and partition of the Koreas, the breakup and reunion of Vietnam, the demolition of the Berlin Wall, and the end of military conscription for all male citizens of service age.

Then in 1991, in a rare gesture of conciliation, North Korea began returning the remains of American service members, including Scott, to the United States, completing the repatriation of more than two hundred combatants by 1994. Most were entrusted to former ambassador and Gov. Bill Richardson of New Mexico, who pulled off a string of diplomatic achievements with the North Korean regime in those days. Because of Korea's cold, dry climate, the remains came back in very good condition. But identifying them was difficult because the dead soldiers had been jumbled together in mass graves, their remains commingled, and they had been recovered by North Koreans, not by the American specialists who have developed expertise at such operations, which are conducted with the precision and thoroughness of an archaeological dig. Identification was further complicated because much of the documentary material normally available through service records, such as medical files and dental charts, was destroyed in 1973, when a fire swept through the National Personnel Records Center outside St. Louis. That conflagration wiped out the files of 16 to 18 million citizens who served between 1912 and 1963, many of them in the Korean conflict.

Thus for A. V. Scott and hundreds who served with him, what should have been a routine matter of matching military records with remains became a painstaking chore of many years. Finding names to fit the bones was the responsibility of the Joint POW/MIA Accounting Command (JPAC), a branch of the Department of Defense which has recovered and identified hundreds of service members from conflicts dating as far back as the Civil War. Scott's unidentified remains, stored on a shelf at JPAC's forensic laboratory at Hickam Air Force Base in Hawaii, remained in limbo for another two decades until scientists, working through veterans' groups and family networks, tracked down Scott's cousins in Detroit, drew mitochondrial DNA samples from them, and declared a match for the corporal in June 2011.[2]

By this time, Scott's mother, Gladys Caldwell, had been dead for fifteen years, never knowing her son's fate. He had gone to war with other members of the largely African-American 503rd Battalion and simply vanished.[3] "She didn't talk about him a lot," said Rudolph L. Caldwell, seventy, Scott's half-brother and closest living relative. "It really bothered her. It tore her apart. It's something that haunted the family, not having a funeral and not knowing what happened."[4]

Caldwell and a handful of surviving relatives made the trip

from Detroit to Arlington for Scott's funeral on September 1, 2011, lined up by the corporal's grave, and listened to the ritual reading of Scripture and the crack of rifles, which provided a long-deferred sense of closure and a measure of comfort for the family. Caldwell lamented his mother's absence. "It would have meant the world to her," he said as the half-brother he had barely known took his place on the front row of Section 60. Corporal Scott went into the ground a few weeks after his right-hand neighbor at Arlington, Army Spec. Daniel L. Elliot, twenty-two, was killed by an IED in Iraq and buried; and a few days before Army Col. Charles Patrick Murray, a veteran of World War II, Korea, and Vietnam, and a Medal of Honor recipient, was buried to Scott's left.

The return of A. V. Scott, along with the steady flow of other repatriations in Section 60, is a reminder of the nation's enduring commitment to its war dead. No other country goes to the effort the United States does to honor its fallen warriors, a national obsession that has its origins in the Civil War. That war, still the deadliest conflict in the country's history, claimed as many as 900,000 lives, with almost half of those going to their graves as unknowns, often without religious rites, a proper coffin, or permanent tombstones. To make up for the debasement suffered by so many in that war, a reunited nation made a conscious decision to do better in the next conflict. When the Spanish-American War ended, specialty teams of investigators, gravediggers, and chaplains were soon dispatched to identify, recover, and repatriate thousands of soldiers, sailors, and Marines from the far-flung battlefields of Cuba, Puerto Rico, and the Philippines. The recovery campaign, accomplished over several years, established the precedent that all combatants killed overseas would be brought home—at government expense—if the next of kin requested it.

With each successive war, the nation has improved its methods of recovering and honoring the dead, issuing the first dog tags in World War I, dedicating Arlington's first Tomb of the Unknown Soldier in 1932, repatriating the first war dead while active hostilities were still under way in Korea in 1951,[5] and establishing a new forensic laboratory at Tan San Nhut Air Base in Saigon in 1966 to improve the speed and accuracy of identifications.

Despite a concerted effort to whittle down the list of lost service members in recent decades, the Defense Department still counts some 80,000 combatants as missing from all wars. Most of these come from World War II (73,000), followed by Korea (8,100), Vietnam (1,600), and the Cold War (126). About half of the missing—some 40,000—are thought to be entombed in wrecks or air crashes so deep at sea that they are beyond recovery.[6]

That was the fate assumed for more than thirty men of the Second Marine Raider Battalion, a pioneering unit that pulled off the first American commando attack of World War II. The Marines' daring raid, against a Japanese garrison on the tiny Pacific island of Butaritari, off Makin Atoll, came in the summer of 1942. Most of the commandos who took part not only survived but won brief fame for a psychological victory at a time when one was sorely needed for the United States in the early stages of war. The amphibious assault on Butaritari, since known to historians as the Makin Island raid, was aimed at destroying a Japanese base deep within enemy territory, gathering intelligence, and diverting Japanese forces from the brawl then unfolding on Guadalcanal and Tulagi to the south.[7]

Some Marine leaders considered the Makin Island raid—the brainchild of the brilliant but eccentric Lt. Col. Evans F. Carlson—to be a "wild and impractical" exploit, but that was exactly its appeal for President Franklin D. Roosevelt. Roosevelt, whose oldest son James was a Marine major and

Carlson's executive officer, loved the idea of an elite unit that could move fast, live off the land, fight hand to hand with Bowie knives, and melt into the night, all of which anticipated the special operations tactics that have become so much a part of recent warfare. The Makin Island raid introduced camouflage fatigues, walkie-talkies, and even the phrase *gung ho* into American culture. The Chinese expression, which Carlson adopted as his battalion's motto, literally means "working together," but in the years since the war, it has come to connote overzealous confidence, in part because of the way the Marines conducted their raid on Makin Island.[8]

There was nothing timid about Carlson's battle plans, which pitted about two hundred well-trained Marines against some eighty Japanese defenders. After weeks of grueling, secretive training in the California mountains, Carlson's Raiders shipped out to Hawaii and transferred to *Nautilus* and *Argonaut*, two mine-laying submarines, for the ten-day voyage to Makin Atoll. There they surfaced offshore in the predawn dark of August 17, 1942, scrambled into rubber dinghies in heavy rains and ten-foot swells, and sloshed ashore as sunrise spread over the Pacific.[9]

Sgt. Clyde A. Thomason, twenty-eight, from Georgia, took the point position for a platoon from B Company and gave his automatic shotgun a little pat. "Okay, Raiders," he said, leading his men across the island, "let's find us a war!" Thomason, a well-regarded Marine with Hollywood good looks and an easygoing style, was first to approach a shack in a taro field, where he kicked in the door, surprised a Japanese soldier inside, and killed him with one blast of double-ought buckshot. Thomason scurried from the building and was soon engaged in a fierce firefight with the main force of Japanese soldiers along the island's primary road.[10]

"It was four minutes of inferno during which everybody in the area was blasting away at somebody or something," said

Sgt. Clyde A. Thomason, at home in Georgia before he won fame for the Marine raid on Makin Island. (Thomason family photo)

Second Lt. Wilfred S. LeFrancois, who led the advance troops from B Company against the Japanese. When the firing sputtered out, scores of enemy dead lay around Marines in the clearing. Then came the crackling of new shooting from high in the surrounding palm trees, where Japanese snipers had set up an ambush.[11]

"He's up there," Thomason shouted to a young Raider who fired into the treetops, which spilled coconuts, palm fronds, and one sniper onto the ground. Thomason, oblivious to the fire still pouring from the trees, paced among his comrades, directing fire and urging his Marines to cover. At six foot three, he made an easy target for the Japanese, who continued plunking away with their Nambu light machine guns until Thomason went down with a thud.[12]

"They got Thomason," a Raider told LeFrancois.[13]

"I inched my way over to him and felt his pulse," LeFrancois recalled.[14] "There was no beat, no more life in this Marine . . . Over his heart appeared a blood stain. It reddened the Marine Corps emblem imprinted on the pocket of his coat."[15] Unable to do anything for his platoon sergeant, LeFrancois returned to the fight, which continued until evening. By the time all was quiet again, the Raiders counted eighty-three Japanese killed, as well as twenty-one of their own.

Because several Japanese planes had swooped over the island that day, the enemy knew about the Marine presence on the atoll and could be expected to return in force to retake Butaritari. Having accomplished the most important part of their mission, Carlson's Raiders collected their dinghies, pushed into a pounding surf, and made for the submarines waiting offshore. High seas and malfunctioning outboard engines hampered the withdrawal, which was chaotic and poorly coordinated. It took the Marines another day, until August 18, to complete their exit.

To avoid a costly reengagement with Japanese forces, the Americans made no attempt to carry Clyde Thomason and other dead comrades to the submarines—it was all they could manage to get the living ones across. So Carlson said a private prayer over each of his comrades, turned each one on his back "that he might rest more easily," and paid a friendly islander fifty dollars to make sure the Marines were properly buried.[16] Then Carlson dashed for the last submarine and began the 2,400-mile run back to Hawaii.[17]

Upon arrival there, Carlson's Raiders had their first opportunity to make a final head count of survivors—and the result was chilling: in their scramble to withdraw from Makin, they had left nine living comrades behind. The nine had been cut off from the main force, and the two companies had been hopelessly mixed together in their desperation to reach the subs. Those on one submarine erroneously assumed that their absent comrades were safe aboard the other. Because both subs maintained radio silence to avoid detection by the Japanese, the mistake was not discovered until a week after the raid. This doomed the men on shore: when Japanese retook the outpost on June 18, they captured the remaining Marines, moved them to nearby Kwajalein Island in the Marshalls, and beheaded them.[18]

The Makin attack also revealed the difficulties inherent in assault by submarine; it was the last time in the war that Marines used subs for such a landing. Finally, the attack almost certainly had the unintended consequence of stiffening Japanese resistance—anticipating determined commando assaults elsewhere, the enemy strongly fortified their positions in the Gilbert Islands, which prolonged the struggle for the Pacific.[19]

Despite these complications, Carlson's Raiders had destroyed the enemy garrison, sunk three Japanese seaplanes, drained aviation fuel supplies, smashed a radio transmitter, and even captured a Rising Sun ensign for their most prominent backer at home, President Roosevelt.[20] "With their raid," said William Douglas Lansford, a former member of the commando unit, "Carlson's Raiders had punctured the myth of the samurai warrior's invincibility ... After a series of Japanese victories at Wake Island, Singapore, Bataan, and Corregidor, Makin was the first Japanese defeat on land."[21]

In the burst of national pride that followed, Carlson won the Navy Cross—and instant hero's status. His Raiders also inspired a Hollywood movie celebrating the attack. The quickly produced film, appropriately entitled *Gung Ho*, hit theaters in 1943, with Randolph Scott in the role of Carlson and a young Robert Mitchum as one of his Raiders. Seen today, the movie seems nakedly propagandistic, but it provided a welcome morale boost at a critical time.[22]

Amie Thomason accepts the Medal of Honor posthumously given to her son,
Sgt. Clyde A. Thomason, in 1943. (Associated Press)

Sergeant Thomason, one of the first Raiders to fall on Makin, posthumously received the Medal of Honor, the nation's highest military tribute, for "conspicuous heroism and intrepidity above and beyond the call of duty . . . in action against the Japanese."²³ In 1943 the Navy brought his step-mother, Amie Maxson Thomason, and two half-brothers to Washington, D.C., for the award, which was presented by James Forrestal, assistant secretary of the navy, and Lt. Gen. Thomas Holcomb, commandant of the Marine Corps. Thomason was the first enlisted Marine to receive the medal in World War II.²⁴

His stepmother, who had raised young Clyde after his biological mother died when he was three, was grateful for the attention, but the main thing she wanted was her son's return from the Pacific. Within a month of his death, she sent his picture and an appeal to the Marine Corps in hopes that it would speed his identification and repatriation. Then she waited. After four months, she received the discouraging news that Sergeant Thomason would not be home soon. "Upon cessation of hostilities," a Marine captain wrote in January 1943, "it is the present intention of the Navy Department to return to this country the remains of Naval personnel who lost their lives in the service of their country, if the next of kin so desire. When it becomes possible to determine the probable date that our dead can be safely removed you will be requested to express your wishes regarding the final disposition to be made of the remains of your stepson."[25]

When the war ended, recovery teams made their way to the atoll in 1946 and again in 1947, interviewed islanders, and came home empty-handed, convinced that the graves would never be found. The island had changed hands several times, bulldozers and other heavy equipment had altered the topography, and investigators abandoned the search for the missing Marines. A military review board rubber-stamped their Makin Island files with a discouraging label: APPROVED NON-RECOVERABLE.[26]

Authorities encouraged Mrs. Thomason to give up waiting. "Although it appears improbable that the remains of your stepson will be recovered," a Marine captain wrote in 1946, "you may be certain that should his remains be positively identified you will be promptly informed and furnished the necessary application blanks to be completed in connection with the return of his remains."[27]

Amie Thomason died at age eighty-five in 1970, still hoping for Clyde's return. With her passing, his cause was taken up by Hugh Maxson Thomason, a half-brother who had been close to the famous Marine, exchanged warm letters with him, practiced saluting with him, and regarded him as a mentor. He had followed Clyde into the Marine Corps, served nine years of active duty, and achieved the rank of colonel in the reserves. Hugh joined forces with survivors of the Makin Island operation to request a new search for the graves on Butaritari Island. He held little hope that his brother's remains could be found and identified after half a century—much less sent home—but even so, he thought it important that someone locate Clyde's grave to settle "a question which now is without answer," and perhaps to place a commemorative marker there to honor "these men who died serving their country."[28]

Pressed by Thomason and members of the U.S. Marine Raider Association, investigators from the Army's Central Identification Laboratory, predecessor agency to JPAC, resumed the search for the lost Raiders in 1998 and 1999, returning to the atoll, now part of the Republic of Kiribati. Although the search teams were armed with maps, accounts of the 1942 raid, and high-tech equipment, including a cesium magnetometer to pinpoint underground anomalies, they had no luck locating the graves. On their third try, in December 1999, a string of interviews led anthropologists to an elderly villager named Bureimoa Tokarei, who spoke no English but knew all the words of the Marine Hymn, which he was happy to sing whenever an American showed up. He also helped solve the mystery of Makin Island, leading investigators to the grave: it was in an old weedy patch among palms, where as a sixteen-year-old boy he had helped bury Carlson's Raiders in 1942.[29] "Experiences like this one confirm that sometimes even the most advanced technology is no substitute for old-fashioned archaeology and the memory of an old man," a member of the team recalled.[30]

Digging within a few yards of where Bureimoa had pointed, investigators uncovered a mass burial six feet deep and eighteen feet long, scattered with skeletons, dog tags, helmets, American hand grenades, canteens, a walkie-talkie, boot fragments, and coins dating no later than 1942. The bones, in remarkably good condition considering their time underground, belonged to nineteen Caucasian males roughly the age and size of the missing Marines; a twentieth skeleton, also from the mass grave, had the structural characteristics of a Pacific islander, most likely a villager executed for murder and ingloriously tossed in with the Marines long after their burial.[31]

Held together by the soil in which they had slept, the skeletons came apart when lifted from the grave, but recovery teams kept each set of remains labeled and boxed separately to preserve their integrity. Bones were then placed in individual caskets, draped with American flags, and carried across the island with due military honors. Loaded aboard a C-130 transport plane, they resumed their long-delayed return to Hawaii.[32] There they were greeted by crowds, a color guard, and old Marines like retired Sgt. Maj. Allan J. Kellogg, Jr., a Medal of Honor recipient who turned out to welcome his brothers home. "Marines are Marines whether or not they are living or dead," he said. "That's the tie that binds us together."[33]

The Raiders then made the short trip from the runway at Hickam Air Force Base to the Army's Central Identification Laboratory, where scientists spent months poring through dental and military records, examining dog tags, sorting bones, and eventually finding names for all nineteen men under their care. No dog tags were found with Clyde Thomason, but his identity was established by his distinctive height, as well as his dental record. Others were identified from DNA samples. A separate batch of mixed bones from the mass grave, most of them fragments from hands and toes, were treated as unidentified remains representing all the dead Raiders.[34]

When the Raiders had been identified, the closest living relatives of each were tracked down and given the option of a private funeral close to home or a group burial in Section 60 at Arlington. Six families chose small private services, while thirteen declared for Arlington, where each of the Raiders would receive a standard white tombstone, with a large marker for the group burial of unidentified remains.[35]

Hugh Thomason had little trouble deciding in favor of Arlington. "It's really quite fitting they will be interred in the same location inasmuch as they shared a common grave for 50 years," he said before the full honors ceremony in Section 60.[36] The services there took place on August 17, 2001, fifty-nine years to the day after Raiders stormed ashore on Makin Island. One by one they came together again under a soft rain and in clinging humidity that evoked their last day fighting in the South Pacific. This time they were welcomed by a thousand well-wishers led by Gen. James L. Jones, commandant of the Marine Corps. Scores of relatives and friends from the U.S. Marine Raider Association also crowded among the tombstones, accepted flags, and heard a Navy chaplain in dress whites offer up an overdue benediction. "Grant that our brothers may sleep in peace until you awaken them in glory," said the chaplain, standing on the grass beside fourteen fresh graves, one for each of the Raiders, one for the group of unidentified warriors.

Bill Giesin, a retired Marine whose uncle and namesake, Pvt. Bill Gallagher, took his place among the dead Raiders at Arlington, found himself strangely moved by the ceremony. "I got a little teary-eyed over a man I never knew," said Giesin, who had spent years writing letters to Congress and badgering the military to bring his uncle home. Giesin had even provided a DNA sample to verify his uncle's identity. "When a man goes so far away to die for his country," said Giesin, "the least his country can do is to make every effort to bring him back."[37]

For his part, Hugh Thomason felt a great sense of relief. "It's been a long time, really, in getting here—and to see the end of all this, why, it's satisfying," he said. As Thomason spoke, the sullen skies parted and the sun broke through, lighting up Section 60 like the stage of a theater. More than a decade after that dramatic moment at Arlington, Thomason, now in his early nineties, remembered the sun instead of the clouds. "Oh, it was special," he said by telephone from Nashville. "It was a bright sunny day, and I was very happy to be there. It is definitely where my brother should be, where he will always be remembered. Yes, I'm sure, that's where he should be."[38]

The Marines had been true to their motto, "Semper Fidelis," Always Faithful, never losing sight of the buddies they had been forced to leave behind. Their homecoming for the dead was a tribute to the persistence of family and friends who never gave up. At the same time, it is unlikely that the Makin Raiders would have been found and returned to Arlington if not for a much later generation of veterans and their families—from the Vietnam era—who shamed the nation into accounting for all service members lost in that unpopular war. In the process, the Vietnam vets raised the standard of care now expected for all soldiers, sailors, airmen, and Marines missing from earlier conflicts.

That transformation, which brought the United States to the forefront of recovering and identifying the war dead, began this way: A few weeks after the Paris Peace Accords ended war between the United States and North Vietnam in January 1973, the first of 672 POWs held by North Vietnam and its allies began flying home—a joyful moment for most families on the receiving end of Operation Homecoming but a wrenchingly disappointing one for those who had sons, fathers, husbands, and brothers among the 2,550 still missing at that point.[39]

Colleen Shine, an eight-year-old then living in Pleasantville, New York, watched with mixed feelings, happy that the planeloads of young warriors were finally coming home, but distraught that her father, Air Force Capt.

Anthony C. Shine, was not among them. Captain Shine, thirty-three, a pilot just beginning his second tour in Vietnam, had been last seen at the controls of his A-7D reconnaissance jet on December 2, 1972, less than a month before the war ended. He had disappeared in the clouds near the border of Vietnam and Laos. His wingman, flying behind Shine in the rugged mountain region, had seen no explosion and no parachute after the captain slipped through the clouds. The wingman heard no distress call on the radio. It was as if Shine, a veteran of more than a hundred combat missions, had simply evaporated. After circling the area to look for wreckage or signs of life on the ground, the wingman carefully noted the location, turned for his home base in Thailand, and reported Shine as missing, a ghostly status he would retain for more than two decades.

On the home front, casualty officials had nothing much to add to this sketchy report of Shine's last moments. All the Air Force could say with certainty was that Anthony "Tony" Shine was gone, officially neither alive nor dead. "My mother didn't know if she was a wife or a widow for twenty-four years," Colleen Shine recalled.[40] In large part, this was because a wall of silence fell over Vietnam in the years following the war. The victorious enemies of the United States demonstrated no interest in helping Americans recover their compatriots. The U.S. government, eager to consign a divisive conflict to the past, made very little effort to press Vietnam for more information. Until relations were reestablished between the two nations in 1995, Americans had no way to search crash sites or old battlegrounds for missing comrades, to learn how they had died, or to determine if by some miracle they were still alive. Families like Shine's were plunged into a long twilight of uncertainty, not knowing whether to grieve for the dead or to entertain hope that a loved one might walk through the front door again.

"You can't put the war behind you," Colleen said, recalling her family's years of uncertainty. "You can't go forward. You are stuck between two worlds." [41] While there is nothing good about having a loved one killed in action, it is in some ways preferable to having one missing. "Uncertainty is a whole different burden," she said. "You don't have a truth to face and move forward from."[42]

For the Shine family, that burden was made heavier by another recent loss: Tony's youngest brother, Army First Lt. Jonathan Shine, had been killed in a firefight in Vietnam in 1970. At least his remains had been recovered and brought home to the cemetery at West Point, where he had so recently graduated as a young officer, eager for the fight. The family wrestled with that loss, along with Tony's disappearance, amid the cultural wars of the 1970s, in which they were viewed as outcasts by some fellow citizens. "It was really hard on my mom," said Colleen. "She had no husband. She had three kids to raise. People were spitting on her because my dad had been flying in Vietnam. They threw Coke bottles at her. They called him a baby killer. And they teased me at school when I handed out MIA leaflets on the playground. Our government told us to keep quiet. They didn't want us calling attention to the fact that we still had people missing from the war."[43]

Feeling isolated and abandoned by their own government, Shine's family turned inward, relying on one another for support, printing leaflets to be dropped from the air over Vietnam in hopes that witnesses could help find their missing airman. Colleen clung to family pictures, remembered beach rides in her father's battered yellow Jeep, and read his last letter again and again. Written six days before he disappeared, it was not a generic "Dear Family" dispatch but was meant especially for Colleen and written in the clear strong hand Tony had acquired while recovering from polio as a child.[44] "Thank you for your last letter honey," he wrote from his base in Thailand. "I sure like to get mail from my family." The letter continued:

> Mom says you kids really like your new school and that you are in the best reader group. That is super and I'm proud of you. It's hard to believe it is winter in New York and snowing. I want you Shannon and Anthony to be careful this winter and not go near the ice on the lake unless Mom is with you or says it's okay. Ice that looks good can sometimes break . . . I am not going to send you kids Christmas presents in the mail from Thailand. I will bring some things home with me when I come. We can have a party when I get there. I love all you kids and miss you very much. Love Dad.[45]

"That was the last time I heard from him," Colleen recalled years later, "so I held on to that letter." As the years passed, she and other members of the family also held to the idea that there were answers to her father's whereabouts if they just kept searching. "We were a military family," said Colleen. "The Warrior Ethos carried us forward. And we met other people who were going through the same experience. That made us feel less isolated."[46] The Shines found solace in the National League of POW/MIA Families, a newly emerging political power, which pressed the government for answers, called attention to POW/MIA issues in newspaper and television interviews, testified before congressional committees, and organized high-visibility rallies around Washington. "I remember the first time I saw the White House was with a 'President Carter, Where's My Daddy?' sign in my hand," said Colleen. She kept asking that question.

After graduating from Wellesley College in 1986, she went to work as public relations director for the National League of Families, which grew into an eloquent voice for missing service members. "We thought our government wasn't doing enough to find these men who had sacrificed everything," she said. "We pushed them to do the right thing, to give a full accounting of what happened to my dad and all the others."[47]

As relations between the United States and Vietnam began to thaw in the 1980s, new reports from refugees and other witnesses began flowing in from Asia—a rusty dog tag found here, a bit of plane wreckage discovered there, a burly POW glimpsed in the Laotian jungle. Few of these tantalizing sightings had credibility, but each had to be verified or debunked. Colleen, taking over her mother's role as the family's point person on POW/MIA matters, scrutinized every report from Vietnam, prowled the halls of Congress, and politely but doggedly badgered the government to keep searching for her father. She pressed apathetic and sometimes incompetent American officials to follow up with witnesses and master the details of their MIA investigations. "I needed them to do it well, and I knew it better than they did," Colleen told an interviewer. "He was my father, not theirs."[48]

Because of pressure from Colleen and like-minded advocates in the POW/MIA community, Congress took an increasing interest in the fate of missing service members. It also helped that Vietnam veterans such as John McCain, John Kerry, Chuck Hagel, and others had won election to Congress, where they helped win new federal funds for search and recovery operations in Vietnam, Laos, and Cambodia. This led to the establishment of a new, expanded POW/MIA office, known as the Joint Task Force Full Accounting, in the Defense Department. The task force established contacts in Southeast Asia, beefed up its staff, collected case files, and began chasing leads. They were soon recovering the first remains of Vietnam-era service members at scattered crash sites and battlefields throughout the region.

Finally, in 1994, the Shine family's perseverance paid off. A joint team of American and Vietnamese researchers located a crash site near Tony Shine's last known location, not far from the Laotian border in Nghe An Province of Vietnam. A local villager claimed to have witnessed the crash of Shine's plane. He took investigators to the site and showed them a shallow grave, thought to be Shine's. That was the good news. The bad news, conveyed by Air Force casualty officers, was that the crash site had been so heavily scavenged for scrap metal that nothing remained to allow certain identification of Tony's plane. And the grave had been looted, leaving a handful of scattered bone fragments too meager for the DNA testing then available. "They said any other remains would have been washed away by floods or destroyed by acidic soil," Colleen said.[49] "Unfortunately our family was told there was nothing further our government could do."[50]

Having spent most of her life searching for her father, Colleen Shine had come up against a dead end. She was on the point of giving up after twenty-two years in this crusade, but before she did, she wanted to try one last, desperate throw of the dice: she would go to Vietnam, find the place her father had died, speak to any witness she could track down, and finish her quest there, whatever the outcome. "If there's anything further I can do on the case I will," she reasoned. "And if there isn't, I'll have to come away knowing I have to move on with my life, that I don't want to spend every minute of the rest of my life trying to do this."[51]

Before relations between the United States and Vietnam were fully in place, Colleen won special permission from both countries to visit Vietnam in February 1995. She rented a Soviet jeep, hired a driver, found an interpreter, and headed over washboard roads for Huu Kiem, a remote mountain village near her father's crash site. There she found a Vietnamese known only as Mr. Quynh, who had witnessed Tony Shine's plane crash in 1972. Mr. Quynh, an ethnic Thai gentleman in flip-flops, led his American visitor up a steep, slippery mountain trail to the ravine where the metal pieces of an airplane were strewn across the jungle. Colleen began collecting shards of metal, some with serial numbers still visible on them. She sat at the grave where her father's remains had been buried and looted. She cried. She borrowed a battered flight helmet that Mr. Quynh had collected from the crash site and promised to return it if it did not prove to be her father's. Back at her car, turning the helmet in her hands, she looked inside and almost fainted. There, handwritten in block letters in faded black ink on a side panel of the helmet, she saw the letters: SHINE. The American investigators had seen the same helmet on their visit to Huu Kiem. They had taken twenty-three photographs of it. And they had told the family that there was nothing to link it with Shine's crash. They had never bothered to look inside.[52]

Colleen returned home, kept the helmet, and displayed it in meetings with officials at the State Department, the Defense Department, and in a session with President Bill Clinton. This led to her meeting with Gen. John Shalikashvili, chairman of the Joint Chiefs of Staff. She took the helmet to Capitol Hill, where she wielded it as a weapon against the inept performance of the investigators who had bungled their assignment in Vietnam. Her teaching tool proved effective. A few weeks after her session on the Hill, a shamefaced Defense Department ordered a new team of investigators back to Vietnam for a full excavation of Shine's crash site. This time they found airplane parts with serial numbers matching his plane, a dog tag stamped with his name, and pieces of a human clavicle, vertebrae, and finger bones. The remains just filled a ziplock bag, but it was enough for a new method of DNA testing by mitochondrial sampling. Scientists at the Armed Forces DNA Identification Laboratory in Rockville, Maryland, comparing mitochondrial DNA from the crash site with blood samples from Tony Shine's mother and siblings, found a match. The bones belonged to Tony Shine, who was soon on his way to Arlington for a funeral that many had thought would never

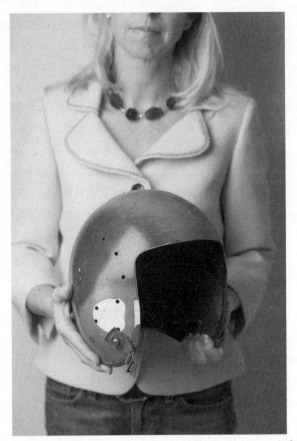

Colleen Shine holds her father's helmet, the result of a long search following his disappearance in Vietnam. (Bruce Weller)

take place. It happened on October 11, 1996, complete with a horse-drawn caisson, a marching band, and a eulogy from Shine's only surviving brother, Army Col. Alexander P. Shine, a veteran of two combat tours in Vietnam.[53]

Colonel Shine, presiding at the main chapel at Fort Myer, just beyond the gates to the cemetery, acknowledged his family's frustration with the government, but he noted that "any discontent with our own government, where it exists, is at the margin, not the heart of the matter. In the long struggle for a full accounting we have never doubted that the real enemy is in Hanoi, not Washington." Looking out over the crowd, which included the Air Force chief of staff and other dignitaries, he thanked those who had brought his brother home from Vietnam. "What is truly remarkable today is that a ceremony like this is taking place at all," Shine said. "After all, we are only talking about 2,500 or so men [missing from the Vietnam War]. They are men whose usefulness to the U.S. government has long since passed, and all but a few are undoubtedly long dead. Most nations in history would simply write them off and get on with other things. But for over twenty years our government has spent vast resources and devoted considerable human efforts to win the freedom—or the return of a few bones—of men like Tony Shine. Why do we do this? Because for all its imperfections our government is still a government of the people, by the people, and for the people. The American people care, and so do those we elect to high office. We are profoundly thankful to be Americans, and that we may lay to rest Tony's few earthly remains beneath the soil of the land he loved and for which he willingly sacrificed his life."[54]

When Colonel Shine was finished, an Air Force honor guard carried his brother's flag-draped casket outside to the waiting caisson, where six stout bay horses, perfectly aware of their role in the proceedings, tossed their heads and stomped their hooves, eager to get moving. The honor guard slowly slid the casket into place and snugged down the colors, and a brass band struck up a rousing version of the Air Force Hymn, which asks the Lord to "guard and guide the men who fly / Through the great spaces of the sky." The horses eased forward, and the long queue of mourners fell in line, following the creaking caisson past the gates to the thump of drums, down the long, familiar course into the cemetery. Tony's widow, Bomette "Bonnie" Shine, led the mourners, followed by Colleen, who had done so much to bring this moment into being, and by Tony's other two children. The three kids, now grown, had never been far from their father's influence, despite his long absence. "Even all the time he was gone, my dad was front and center in my family," Colleen said. "We talked about him all the time. We wanted to find out what happened to him. And we were trying to live by the values for which he was willing to die—integrity, loyalty, courage."[55]

When the procession arrived in Section 60, eight members of the honor guard stepped up, slipped Shine's casket from the caisson, and carried him to the grave, where a chaplain murmured the old words of comfort. Bonnie, sitting on the front row, watched a matched team of neatly pressed airmen carefully fold the flag she had waited nearly twenty-four years to accept. Just as she did so, four F-15 fighter jets came screaming over the cemetery in tight formation. One plane peeled off from the others, shot straight up into the sky like a rocket, and left a gap among the remaining jets to represent their absent comrade, a final gesture of respect for Lt. Col. Anthony C. Shine.

Colleen still comes to Section 60 with her own children, with whom she shares stories about her father's long journey from Vietnam. "That story is so much a part of who we are. It defines our family," she said, looking around at the new tombstones planted in all directions from her father's grave, which anchors the central part of Section 60. "It's so serene here," she said on a recent visit. "It's a place my dad's buddies can visit. It's where people from different wars find that they have things in common. Everybody here has lost somebody, everybody knows the value of that folded flag, everybody's struggling to get on with their lives. When I meet the widows and children who've lost loved ones in Iraq and Afghanistan, I tell them my own presence here is proof that you can get through this."[56]

Despite the setbacks and blunders that frustrated Colleen's quest, the government learned from its mistakes, improved its

Colleen Shine with a photograph of her father and the A-7D jet he flew in Vietnam. (Bruce Weller)

methods, and developed new expertise in its treatment of the war dead. Hundreds of lost service members have been repatriated from Southeast Asia since Tony Shine came home. His recovery, and others like his, have inspired veterans of earlier wars to seek similar honors for their missing comrades. Under pressure from the public, Congress has expanded its mandate for the Joint POW/MIA Accounting Command, which has taken on responsibility for MIAs from Korea (1994), for service members lost over New Guinea in World War II (1999), and for all others missing from World War II (2009). What was once a tiny wartime morgue at Tan San Nhut Airbase has grown into the world's largest forensic laboratory at Hickam Air Force Base in Hawaii, where more than five hundred civilian anthropologists, historians, analysts, and military personnel work alongside one another today, scouring old crash sites and battlefields, providing missing warriors with an identity, and giving a place for them to rest with honor.[57]

"It's the least we can do," said Colleen.[58]

8

FINAL HONORS

F EW PEOPLE EVER forget an Arlington funeral, not only because it marks an important passage, but also because of the care and decorum with which young men and women from the military carry out farewell rituals for one of their own.

Each branch of the armed forces fields specially trained honors teams at Arlington, where brushed and polished comrades convey the dead to their graves, fold flags, and fire rifle salutes. They snap to attention for the final sounding of Taps, which echoes among the tombstones more than twenty times a day. The old ritual is played out again and again throughout the year—down by the river in Section 60 for those killed in recent action, elsewhere in the cemetery for retirees who have earned a place at Arlington.[1] Like most rituals, these unfailingly follow the same well-tempered choreography, brought to perfection by long hours of drilling and preparation.

Members of the Old Guard's Caisson Platoon carry service members for final honors in grand style. (Sgt. Lustino Brooks)

For the fifty-six soldiers and sixty-plus horses of the Old Guard's Caisson Platoon, work begins long before sunrise, as preliminaries for the day's funerals get under way. By four A.M., the lights are blazing at Fort Myer Stables, a complex of aged redbrick buildings where bleary-eyed soldiers in jeans and boots muck the stalls, fork the hay, and wash the sturdy horses assigned for cemetery duty, a collaboration between man and beast with origins in the Civil War.

"The biggest thing you need here is the work ethic," said Staff Sgt. T. J. Goodman, the ranking noncommissioned officer of the platoon, who steps back to make way for horses clomping to the washing room. "Our guys start work before anybody else, and they keep at it all day. This is a high-visibility mission—everybody's watching, from the time you leave in the morning until you come back in the afternoon—so you have to look good, watch your posture in the saddle, and keep your horses looking good. It's a sign of respect for the service members and their families."[2]

Sgt. Eric Wies washes Omar in preparation for a day of funerals.
(Sgt. Lustino Brooks)

As Goodman spoke, seven horses from the white team were led one by one from the wash stalls to a dimly lit aisle where each was brushed, combed, and tied by a halter outside its box, while horses from the black team filed down the line for their turn in the showers.[3] At the far end of the stables, meanwhile, the tack room was filling with the heady scent of leather polish and Brasso, as soldiers cleaned bridles and harnesses, buffed their uniform buttons to a high sheen, and put a final shine on their riding boots, all the while with an eye on the clock, which signaled that it was almost time to change from work clothes to dress blues, already pressed and hanging in plastic sheaths nearby.

By seven A.M., two spotless black caissons, both relics of World War I, rattled through the Fort Myer gates and into the cemetery, one wagon powered by six gray horses, the other by six dark bays. This configuration dated to Civil War days, with all six animals harnessed in pairs and saddled, the latter a precaution that allowed horses to be easily removed and ridden off during battle. Traditionally the wagons carried ammunition and cannons to the front and returned with dead or injured soldiers, a practice that naturally led to the use of caissons for the first funerals at Arlington National Cemetery. These days three soldiers rode mounted on three harnessed horses on the left-hand side of each wagon, while a section sergeant set the pace, riding out front untethered to the caisson. The sergeant and his mount, usually a big bruiser the other horses respect, called the shots. Each team heading into the cemetery was trailed at a discreet distance by a soldier in a white truck. Known as a section worker, he carried lunch for the team, water buckets, lead ropes, lint rollers, shoe polish, spare buttons, hoof picks, curry combs, and other paraphernalia to keep horses and riders going all day. He also wielded a shovel, clearing Arlington's roadways of the copious fertilizer the horses drop between—and sometimes during—funerals.

"What did you do to get this duty?" someone asked the soldier with the shovel.

"It's part of a rotation," said the specialist, who would be on horseback for his next assignment. "This job isn't so bad, especially on a day like this." He waved a hand at the blazing heat and humidity of another Washington summer. "The other soldiers are sweating while I'm driving around with air conditioning."[4]

Arlington can be unbearable in summer, especially if you are standing in direct sunlight at strict attention in your dress blues with your coat buttoned to the choking point while a minister drones on, far exceeding the five minutes normally allotted for the ecclesiastical part of an Arlington ceremony. "So you stay hydrated and try to hang on," said Staff Sgt. William Whitley, who watched a casket team from his unit, the Old Guard's H Company, practicing in the shade behind the barracks on Sheridan Drive at Fort Myer. "One of our soldiers had a thermometer in his pocket the other day, and it registered 125 degrees." Whitley stood with other soldiers around a picnic table, not far from a gas grill that would be fired up for hamburgers a few hours later. On top of the picnic table was a battered oak practice casket from the York Casket Co., the focus of Whitley's team. They would lift it, carry it, set it down, fold and unfold flags over it, and repeat the procedure again and again as the morning wore on. They worked slowly, lugging the box to a spot in the courtyard and lowering it to the ground, just as they would for real funerals when they returned to cemetery duty next week. This box rattled because it carried 180 pounds of flat iron weights, placed inside to simulate human cargo.[5]

Whitley, an affable North Carolinian dressed informally in cammies for the drill session, offered a steady stream of advice to those lined up on each side of the casket. "Step a little bit closer to the casket," he told a private whose end of the box had wobbled when he lifted it from the table. "It's easier to hold it that way." "Your feet were good that time," he told another man, "but the front was low. You had the casket level this way but not that way." He tilted his hand to indicate the angles. "Take it back," he said, urging them to return the casket to the picnic table and repeat the journey. "Take it back," he said, ordering another round trip. "Take it back—you'll hear that phrase more than anything in the Old Guard," he told a visitor. "You practice and practice until the muscle memory takes over and you don't have to think about it—it's like shooting baskets."

Whitley's team carried the casket until they had the pace just right, making sure the box rode on the level from the moment it came off the table (about the height of a caisson or a hearse) until they eased it down onto the ground. Then came flag folding, practiced over the casket while the morning traffic, heading for Washington, whooshed by on U.S. Route 50 a few yards outside the Fort Myer gates. One soldier folded his end of the flag neatly but bungled the transfer to the man across from him. "You jumped on the hand-off," Whitley barked. "Catchers, don't reach. Wait for it to come to you. Gonzales, slow down your fold orders. You're going too fast. Werner, stop that smiling. Try again."

Catchers, draggers, folders, and presenters kept at it around the outstretched flag, repeating the thirteen-step folding ceremony again and again until the slow-motion procedure looked smooth and effortless, as if accomplished by a single organism. It was something of a magic trick, transforming the well-known red, white, and blue rectangle into a tight blue triangle with only stars showing. That was how the ensign should be handed to the family, which would never unfurl it.

After several runs of folding and unfolding, the casket team seemed to satisfy Whitley. "There," he said. "Good to go!" The young soldiers took the training in stride, turning serious when lugging the casket or folding the flag, their faces drained of emotion, eyes fixed on the middle distance. Between training bouts, however, they joked freely around the casket with all the exuberance of youth. "It's grab-ass and joking out here," said Whitley, "but when they step off the bus at Arlington, it's like somebody hits a switch. They hit the ground stone-faced, all business."

Whitley ordered a break in the practice session, and a cherubic young soldier named Purcell peeled off from the group, walked over to a visitor, and unabashedly expressed pride in Company H. "You will find that we are the best, sir," he said, his buddies nodding agreement. It was not long before he was back with the casket team, which resumed its heavy lifting, slow-marching, and flag folding, this time to the accompaniment of gunfire, which echoed off the brick walls of the barracks.

Just around the corner another Old Guard specialty unit—a firing party—was drilling for its part of the funeral ritual. Young soldiers in battle dress uniform crowded onto a service road alongside U.S. Route 50, grabbed a handful of blank 7.62-millimeter rifle cartridges from an ammunition box, loaded their M-14 weapons, and got down to business. Like carrying caskets and folding flags, firing salutes requires close coordination and fluidity of movement.

"You want all members of the firing party on the same page, doing the same thing," said Staff Sgt. Jake France, overseeing his platoon. "When they render the volley, it should sound like one shot, not a ripple of shots. And all the weapons should be lined up at the same angle." Each firing party consists of seven riflemen and a sergeant like France, who called orders for the traditional three-rifle volley that paves the way for Taps at every honors funeral.

Members of an Old Guard firing party practice at Fort Myer.
(Sgt. Lustino Brooks)

Out behind the barracks, the seven-soldier squad filed into position, dressing its line so that each man stood an arm's length from his neighbor. Staff Sgt. France watched them critically as they cycled through the rifle-handling exercise known as the manual of arms, from "port arms" to "present arms" to "order arms," with the soldier at the middle of the line calling out each step, "One, two, three . . . one, two, three," the men shifting feet, hands, and rifles in synchrony.

"I can barely hear you," France told the man calling the count.

"Your glove should be below your left eye," he told another.

"Close your mouth."

"Focus on your foot separation."

"Okay, let's do it again."

A firing party from the Old Guard's H Company renders a final salute at Arlington. (Staff Sgt. Megan Garcia)

"Attention!" he said.

The firing party stiffened.

"Ready."

The line of men, at port arms, pivoted 45 degrees, racked a round into their rifles, and slapped the wrist of their weapons simultaneously.

"Aim."

Each man swung his rifle to eye level, barrels kicking into place like a line of Rockettes.

"Fire."

Gunshots cracked the morning air, prompting a frown from France.

"Too much of a ripple," he said. "That sounded like two shots. Should be just one. Let's do it again. Ready!"

They repeated the exercise . . . Ready, Aim, Fire! again and again, each iteration producing a new barrage of criticism from the sergeant.

"You didn't have total control of your weapon when you were doing your rack."

"You need to watch your foot separation."

"Stop fucking talking!"

"You've got the wrong angle at port," he said. "The butt should be at your hip and the barrel here by your face."

"All right, let's do it again," he said, drilling the team until their volleys spoke as one.

"We rate each volley on a scale of one to four," France said, "with one as the worst and four being perfect."

"That last one sounded perfect," someone said.

"A three at best," said France, who went back to drilling, walking over a carpet of spent brass cartridges piling up on the pavement, a few yards across U.S. Route 50 from a Days Inn motel. Hotel patrons, awakened by a fusillade so close at hand, have been known to crack their curtains and peer cautiously across the road to locate the source of the ruckus.

"We try not to start too early," said France, with a hint of a smile.[6]

There were no smiles a few days later when the casket team and firing party filed from their buses and onto the turf in Section 60, silently took up their positions around a fresh grave, and crisply executed final honors for a soldier just killed in Afghanistan. The Old Guard, smartly turned out in their dress blues, sailed through the ceremony without a hitch, the casket team marching smoothly over the grass, the firing party setting up its line about fifty yards from the gravesite to provide mourners a comfortable buffer from the noise. On a signal from graveside, the soldiers popped off a perfect three-rifle volley aimed over the grave. Some believe that the din, along with the smell of cordite, paves the way for a warrior's arrival in the afterlife, like firecrackers at a Chinese funeral.

All religious faiths—and even the lack of any belief at all—are honored at Arlington, which provides Catholic, Protestant, and Jewish chaplains for families who want them and follows guidelines from the U.S. Department of Veterans Affairs for the religious symbols allowed on tombstones. Walking among the graves in Section 60 is an ecumenical experience, with a dizzying assortment of religious emblems incised over the names of dead Methodists, Presbyterians, Episcopalians, Lutherans, Moravians, Unitarians, Christian Scientists, Mormons, Seventh Day Adventists, Russian Orthodox, Greek Orthodox, and members of the Church of World Messianity, each with its distinctive emblem. A few stones have a blank space instead of religious symbols, while others announce their faiths with the Jewish Star of David, the Buddhist Wheel of Righteousness, the Sikh Khanda, or two-edged sword, the Baha'i nine-pointed star, the Native American teepee, and the Muslim crescent and star. The Wiccan symbol, once a magnet for controversy, appears on at least two tombstones in this part of Arlington.[7]

Spec. Charles Thomas Heinlein's grave is marked by the Wiccan pentacle,
one of many religious icons on display in Section 60. (Robert M. Poole)

The Wiccans' five-pointed star, or pentacle, sometimes misconstrued as a satanic icon, arrived in Arlington only after a prolonged legal battle brought by relatives of dead soldiers and the American Civil Liberties Union, which argued that service members should be allowed to display the symbol as a matter of free speech protected by the First Amendment. The Veterans Administration, which sets standards for 131 national cemeteries under its jurisdiction, viewed the Wiccans with suspicion—after all, many had identified themselves as witches and pagans. But after several decades of stalling and under threat from the ACLU, the VA finally came down on the side of religious tolerance, agreeing to display the pentacle symbol in 2007.[8]

"If you've been to war and done what these young men have done, you should have anything you want on your tombstone," said Tom Heinlein of Hemlock, Michigan, who stood before the grave of his son, Spec. Charles Thomas Heinlein, Jr., in Section 60. The younger Heinlein, a Wiccan awarded the Bronze Star and Purple Heart for his service in Iraq, was killed by an IED in Baghdad in August 2007, a few months after the Wiccans won the right to show their symbols on government-issued tombstones.[9] "I honor my son's beliefs, which did no harm to anybody," said the elder Heinlein, a round man in a black T-shirt who had come to visit his son for Memorial Day. "All these guys are all the same." He gestured toward the tombstones pressing around him. "They all did what they were supposed to do. They all deserve to be here."[10]

Nothing can soften the shock of losing a loved one in wartime, but there is some consolation in knowing that you will not face the death alone. Every service assigns uniformed casualty officers to break the bad news to the next of kin—in person—within hours of a combatant's death; casualty officers steer families through plans for a military funeral if one is desired; and members of the honor guard take charge of their dead comrades at Arlington, see that they are treated respectfully, and remain with them until the final notes of Taps ring over the tombstones.

"We're right there with the family, a few feet in front of them," said Staff Sgt. Alfredo Caballero, a member of the Air Force casket team with more than a year of funerals under his belt. "We're close enough to smell the perfume and hear the sobbing. It gets very personal."[11]

On the family side of the grave, a journey to Arlington is fraught with emotion, which finds a thousand ways of expression: mistresses jostle with wives for position on the front row, estranged siblings renew old arguments, and parents are sorely tested by the presence of in-laws they detest.

"She was a nutbag and heavily medicated and a pain in the ass," said a distraught father, referring to his dead son's widow, who sat two chairs away from him at a recent funeral. "We weren't speaking to her."[12]

The mother of a dead Marine was so exasperated by her daughter-in-law's appearance at her son's Arlington funeral that she was still sputtering about it several years later. "I don't know why she even bothered to come!" said the mother, who confirmed that her son's widow was seven months pregnant by another man at the time. The widow took center stage at the funeral and accepted her husband's flag. She was deeply resented by Marines on honors detail, who knew the score but carried out their mission with icy professionalism.[13]

"We don't take sides," said Master Sgt. Christopher D. Albright, who directed hundreds of Marine funerals at Arlington before retiring in 2013. "We're there to honor the Marine and to support his family. Things can get pretty emotional. I've met fathers who look at you like they hate everything you stand for, like they hold you responsible for a son's death. Me, I've learned to be pretty stoic at times like that. You have to maintain decorum." Like others assigned to duty at Arlington, Marines are expected to remain impassive, fold the flags, and stand tall for those whose lives are falling apart around the grave.

Service members take extraordinary care in their appearance for funerals, keeping their uniforms pressed and spotless for ceremonial duty, with seams straight, shoes polished, and medals aligned to the thousandth of an inch. Likewise, most families rise to the occasion. They usually turn up at Arlington in their Sunday best, in suits, ties, and sober dresses. But others come to say their farewells in Hawaiian shirts, flip-flops, shorts, jeans, T-shirts, spandex, or some combination of the above. One casket team, expecting to carry a comrade's ashes

Lance Cpl. Ruben Franco, a Marine Body Bearer, puts a final crease in the flag at Arlington ceremonies. (Cpl. Mondo Lescaud)

in a bronze urn, was surprised to find him sealed in a container shaped like a cowboy boot; another was brought to Arlington in an urn made to look like G.I. Joe. Not much rattles old regulars like Albright, who has learned to be ready for anything. "At this point," he said, "we've seen it all."[14]

The constant exposure to sudden death and nonstop grieving at Arlington takes a toll on those assigned to the front lines. "Two or three years is about the max for this duty," said Lt. Jonathan Bush, a Navy chaplain who has performed more than fifteen hundred funerals at Arlington. "I can still picture everyone who was at every funeral." Bush has seen a long parade of pilots, infantrymen, and Navy SEALs into the ground in recent years. "It's never easy, but I try to provide some comfort to the family and friends. I tell them not to dwell on how this person died, but how he lived. And I encourage them to live their lives in a way that honors that Marine or sailor." Faced with the death of a young warrior, Bush finds it difficult to explain why one person lives and another dies. "I don't have the answers," he said, walking among the graves in Section 60. "I hope to find out someday."[15]

Like others on the funeral beat, Bush admitted the difficulty of maintaining martial composure when children appear on the front row, somewhat bewildered by the experience. "That's the toughest," said Lance Cpl. Ruben Franco, one of the hulking Marines of Bravo Company, who has carried countless comrades to their graves in Section 60. "You're standing there holding the flag, and this little kid's crying, 'Where's Daddy? Where's Daddy? Why is he in the hole?' Man, that gets to you! But we can't let it show."[16]

Franco and other body bearers fend off the stress with three-mile runs and long hours of pumping iron at the Marine Corps Barracks at Eighth and I Streets, S.E., in Washington, where Marines have held the ground since 1801. By 7:30 on a recent spring morning, the casket detail was already at work, carrying trash cans loaded with weights through the dim recesses of a basement parking lot at the barracks, slow-marching with heavy practice caskets, and folding flags with a delicacy incongruous in men who would not look out of place on the defensive line of an NFL team.

"Our guys average 250 pounds," said Cpl. Brian Bell, the noncommissioned officer guiding the body bearers through their morning routine. "Everybody here is at least six feet tall. We recruit Marines for this assignment and put them through rigorous training before they're ready for a funeral." After fifty-seven days of ceremonial drill school, candidates for assignment as body bearers must pass a demanding physical test, bench-pressing 225 pounds, seat-pressing 135 pounds, curling the straight bar with 115 pounds, squat-lifting 315 pounds, and dead-lifting 315 pounds. "Then you come here," said Bell, studying cropped and heavily muscled colleagues lugging trash cans and wrestling with heavy caskets, part of a two-hour session that precedes each day's funerals.

Marines from Bravo Company bear a comrade among the tombstones at Arlington. A plastic cover protects the flag from rain. (Cpl. Austin Hazard)

Proud of doing more with less, the Marines assign six people to each casket detail, three to a side. Other services use eight people, four to a side. "That's what makes Marines different—we do everything a bit differently," said Bell, one of fourteen body bearers on duty in Washington. He watched his team folding a flag in exaggerated slow motion, which the Marines call "ceremonious speed," with none of the snap and pop that the Army and Air Force bring to the same task. "We slow down the tempo, take our time." Bell explained that this was a way to express sadness at a fallen comrade's absence.

For the same reason, the body bearers walk the dead to the grave with a deliberate, smooth catch-step that is positively balletic: on some days at Arlington, if you glimpse them from a distance, they appear to be skating among the tombstones, guiding a brother- or sister-in-arms toward the smoothest of landings. At graveside, where a brass band offers up a very slow version of the Marine Hymn, the body bearers file into position, take three steps in place, and in a final salute to the dead, hoist his casket to eye level. They hold it there, a bit closer to heaven, until the last notes of the song melt away. Then they softly lower it over the grave. They make it look easy.

"You don't know how much weight is in the casket until you step up to it and lift," said Corporal Bell, "so we're ready for anything, physically as well as mentally. We've had high winds that threatened to take the flag away, broken handles on the casket, and really bad weather. The only way a funeral can be called off is if the family decides to call it off."[17]

"It doesn't matter what the conditions are," said Cpl. James Hamby, a body bearer with two combat tours in Iraq and one in Afghanistan behind him, "we'll be there for that Marine. Each funeral has to be perfect." For Hamby and others with combat experience, funeral duty at Arlington is deeply satisfying, just as honorable as service on the firing line. "I was one of the lucky ones who came back. I remember that every time we go to Arlington."[18]

Funerals for young warriors recently killed in action are usually well attended, with scores of mourners flocking to the cemetery. For older veterans the crowds can be depressingly thin.

"We had a service for a World War II Marine the other day," said Lance Cpl. Gary Miller, "and nobody was there. No relatives. No friends. No media. But we still performed for that Marine. We tried to make it perfect, even though nobody was there to see. It's good to know you may get the same treatment someday."[19]

The unwavering order of an Arlington service, with its marching platoons, firing parties, and celebration of warrior culture, strikes some civilians as cold and off-putting. But for more than half a century, this hard-edged martial atmosphere has been softened somewhat by the presence of Arlington Ladies, a volunteer force who, dressed as if they were heading for an afternoon tea, turn up at every funeral with consoling words for surviving friends and family.[20]

Like other traditions at the national cemetery, the tradition of Arlington Ladies began many years ago, purely by happenstance. Gen. Hoyt S. Vandenberg, the chief of staff of the recently created Air Force, was driving through Arlington with his wife, Gladys, in 1948, when they noticed one of their airmen being buried, attended by a lone chaplain and a bugler, with no other well-wishers in sight.

"She vowed that would never happen again—nobody would go to his grave alone," said Jean Anderegg, chairwoman of the Air Force Arlington Ladies today. "Gladys Vandenberg took it upon herself to go to every Air Force funeral to stand in for the family." When the number of funerals increased and it became impossible for Mrs. Vandenberg to cover all of them, she asked friends from the Air Force Officers' Wives Club to pitch in. Thus began the Arlington Ladies Committee, which gradually inspired most of the other services to follow suit with their own versions of Mrs. Vandenberg's squad.

These days an Arlington Lady attends every funeral, making contact with family members before the procession heads for the gravesite. The ladies stand by through the Bible reading, the rifle salutes, and the sounding of Taps, then present a handwritten note of condolence for the next of kin. "I always give them my card and ask them to get in touch if they want to talk," said Anderegg. "It's a terrible moment for families. They are feeling afraid, worried, alone, and sad. So I always give them a smile. And I offer a hand, which they usually grab and hold on to for dear life."

What can one possibly say at such a time?

"We let them know that we're part of the same small Air Force family and that we appreciate every airman's service," said Anderegg. "If I'm talking to parents, I tell them that the Air Force thanks them for raising such a wonderful young man and how deeply sorry we are that we can't bring him home to you."

For Arlington Ladies, as for uniformed members of the honor guard, the recent years have been especially difficult, with war deaths rising and so many new funerals in Section 60. "It's hardest when the kids are there, wondering what is going on. You know this event is going to change their lives forever." To keep from losing her composure, she has trained herself to look for birds among the trees or to study the clouds for the shapes of animals. "All of us have tricks like that—you're going to be strong for those families."

When the bands march off and the crowds scatter, Anderegg and other Arlington Ladies make their way across the grass, always on the arm of a young service member in uniform who politely opens the car door and drives her back to the cemetery's administration building. It looks rather old-fashioned, Anderegg acknowledged, but each Arlington Lady is assigned a funeral escort for good reason.

"It all goes back to the lady in red," she said. Many years ago, in the days before uniformed escorts were part of the ritual, one Arlington Lady arrived for a serviceman's funeral in a bright red dress, hardly appropriate to the occasion. She stood by the grave, innocently waiting for services to begin. The grieving widow arrived, saw the lady in red at graveside, and assumed that she was one of her late husband's mistresses. The widow refused to get out of the car, services were delayed, and the misunderstanding caused unnecessary pain for all involved. Shortly after that, no Arlington Lady went to a funeral without a military escort. "And that's why I always find the husband or wife before the service and explain who I am and why I'm there," said Anderegg.[21]

In the natural evolution of things, as women have risen through the military ranks, a few of their spouses have volunteered for funeral duty as Arlington Gentlemen. Spouses or widowers of officers, they serve without escorts, attending funerals for those in their branch of service. Arlington has become more egalitarian in other ways as well. Women, barred from combat until recently, have nonetheless won assignments that put them in harm's way, as helicopter pilots, nurses, and truck drivers, which has brought several to Arlington in recent years, where they rest alongside their brothers-in-arms. On the other side of the turf, women have also made headway in the ranks of the honor guard, once a domain occupied exclusively by men. Nowadays it is possible, although by no means common, to see women calling the shots for firing parties, marching in platoons, and even carrying the caskets at Arlington.

Staff Sgt. Jennifer Powell, who can lift three hundred pounds, serves on the Air Force casket team, which requires

Staff Sgt. Jennifer Powell, member of the Air Force casket team, once a predominantly male assignment. (Air Force photo)

the same rigorous training her male counterparts endure. "It's an honor to be doing this," she said, chatting between funerals in Section 60, where she had recently steered fellow airmen to rest. "You look at all the graves and realize that this is part of a long tradition—one I'm very proud to be part of. The physical training is challenging—squats, dead lifts, bench press, shoulder press—but the mental discipline is just as vital. We have a saying: 'We vow to stand sharp, crisp, and motionless.' To accomplish that, you have to be focused on keeping your emotions together and getting the mission done."[22]

Like others who have spent long hours in the cemetery, Powell admitted to thinking about her own funeral. "I imagine that I would like to be cremated and then be placed inside a wooden casket," she told *Marine Corps Times*. "That way it's not too heavy . . . But there's just something about having a team carry you."[23]

AFTERWORD

SOME READERS MAY recall one of the worst episodes in the history of Arlington National Cemetery, which came to light in 2009. Over a number of years, more than two hundred graves were misidentified or improperly marked, cremated remains were mishandled, and record keeping haphazard. The cemetery's management was replaced, congressional investigations launched, and new systems put in place to avoid such problems in the future.

Investigators found no evidence of mismanagement in Section 60, but the news caused at least two concerned families to have their sons exhumed from Arlington and positively identified to make sure they were buried in the right place. Both were, and the men were reinterred.

In response to the trauma of misplaced graves, the Department of the Army, which runs the cemetery, thoroughly mapped each of Arlington's 300,000 burials and entered the information into a database that allows administrators to locate every grave within seconds. Visitors can also use the database to find graves by name, using the free ANC Explorer application from Arlington's official website, http://www.arlingtoncemetery.mil.

Seventy soldiers from the Army's Old Guard at Fort Myer were pressed into service for the three-month mapping operation, which began in June 2011 and ended in August. Named Task Force Christman, in honor of Pvt. William Christman, Arlington's first military burial from the Civil War, the soldiers assigned to the project photographed the front and back of every grave with iPhones and tagged each image with GPS coordinates. Soldiers checked to make sure the names on the tombstones matched cemetery records and reported any discrepancies to Arlington's civilian administrators.

"We did the whole thing at night," said Staff Sgt. John McDermott of Delta Company, Third U.S. Infantry Regiment, "to avoid the heat and to make sure we didn't interfere with funerals. We also knew that we'd be able to work more efficiently without interruptions from tourists and visitors curious about what was going on. So we operated after hours, from 1700 hours [five P.M.] until 0600 or 0700, until we got it done." A few soldiers found the idea of stalking the cemetery at night to be a bit creepy, which prompted more than a few ghost stories. One soldier, photographing a grave, felt someone tap him on the shoulder, turned around, and found nobody there; others heard voices and saw ghostly figures moving among the graves.

Such episodes were shrugged off by McDermott and another noncommissioned officer from Delta Company, Staff Sgt. Michael Drake, who attributed the sightings to overactive imaginations. "We knew we'd get stories like that, working at night," said Drake, "but everyone came through the experience all right."[1]

He grieves, he weeps, but then his tears are through.
The Fates have given mortals hearts that can endure.

—HOMER, *The Iliad*, translated by Robert Fagles

ACKNOWLEDGMENTS

I HAVE BEEN wandering among the tombstones in Section 60 for several years, attending services for men and women killed in Iraq and Afghanistan, speaking with comrades who served with them, and passing time with surviving friends and family who come to this part of Arlington to honor loved ones claimed by the nation's longest war. It is also a place of rest for combatants recently repatriated from World War II, Korea, and Vietnam.

I am most grateful to survivors who generously shared their time in Section 60 and to those who exchanged views by e-mail or telephone: Jack and Ann Adams; Rafael and Xiomara Anderson; Joseph Baddick; Regina Barnhurst; Beth Belle; Anthony and Mary Coyer; Paula Davis; Tristan Gale; Becky, Kevin, and Justin Hall; David V. Hill; Tom Heinlein; Jesse Hernandez; Brittany Jacobs; Marine Maj. Jason Johnston; John and Mary Jane Jones; Chaz Kane; Marine Lance Cpl. Brandon Long; Katie Madden; Jim, Brandy, and Alison Malachowski; Chase Martin; Judy Meikle; Yolanda Mercado; Liz, Hayley, and Michael Mocabee; Army Staff Sgt. Christian Mullins; Ami Neiberger-Miller; Marine Sgt. Tim Nunez; Richard and Tammy O'Brien; Glenn Oliver; Sheryl M. Schneider; David

Sharrett; Jill Stephenson; Laura Swink; Carol Ward Thomas; Jean and Hugh Thomason; Susan Ripke; Joe and Rita Rippetoe; Colleen Shine; Army Capt. Chad E. Thibodeau; Thomas Whorl; Vicki Zeigler; and Sue and Megan Zerbe.

The men and women of the Third Infantry Regiment of the Army, better known as the Old Guard, are closely associated with services at Arlington, where they drive the caissons, carry the caskets, fire the salutes, and do so many things to make an Arlington funeral a memorable event. Special thanks to my friend First Sgt. Robert A. Durbin, who served with the elite Honor Guard Company and eased my path with Old Guard soldiers. They generously allowed me to interview them, watch them train, and join them for missions in the cemetery. I am grateful to Lt. James G. Bordelon; Sergeant Maj. Phillip R. Cantrell; Staff Sgt. Michael C. Drake; Maj. Russell H. Fox, Staff Sgt. Adam Eisenhauer; Staff Sgt. T. J. Goodman; Maj. John G. Miller; Staff Sgt. John McDermott; Col. James C. Markert; and Staff Sgt. William Whitley.

The Marines were welcoming and helpful, inviting me to their Washington, D.C., barracks at Eighth and I Streets for training and interviews, as well as their impressive sunset parades. Special thanks to Master Sgt. Christopher D. Albright, former funeral director for the Marine Corps; Capt. John D. Norton; Cpl. Brian Bell; Capt. Eric D. Flanagan; Lance Cpl. Ruben Franco; Cpl. James Hamby; Lance Cpl. Gary Miller; and Capt. Greg Wolf.

From the Air Force, heartfelt thanks to Jean Anderegg, chairwoman of the Air Force Arlington Ladies Committee; Staff Sgt. Alfredo Caballero; Airman First Class Krystal Chase; Col. Charles R. Cornelisse; Technical Sgt. Jennifer A. Lindsay; Lt. Col. Pamela Novy; Lt. Col. Elizabeth A. Ortiz; Staff Sgt. Jennifer Powell; and Capt. Christian L. Williams. I am especially grateful to Maj. Ryan VanVellen, a helicopter pilot and Iraq War veteran who now heads operations for the Air Force Honor Guard at Bolling Air Force Base.

Ed Zeigler, chief of the Navy's public information office in Washington, eased my way with Navy contacts. Lt. Jonathan Bush, who has presided as chaplain for hundreds of Marine and Navy funerals in recent years, spent a good bit of time answering questions and walking through Section 60 with me. I am also grateful to Cdr. Kirk S. Lippold, skipper of the *USS Cole* when Al Qaeda launched one of its first attacks on the United States.

From the Army's Center of Military History, I am grateful to Roderick Gainer, Stephen A. Carney, and Richard Moore, all intimately familiar with the historical importance of the artifacts friends and families leave in Section 60.

All the armed forces cooperated with my research, but my conclusions in no way reflect the official policies of the Army, Air Force, Marines, Navy, or Coast Guard. Any errors are mine alone.

In addition to those mentioned above, I thank Bonnie Carroll, founder and president of the Tragedy Assistance Program for Survivors (TAPS); friend and scholar Terrence M. Doyle; Darcie Sims; and Holly Holman, each of whom contributed in some way to this project.

Thanks to Bruce Dale, a former *National Geographic* colleague who produced the remarkable infrared images of Section 60 for this book. Readers wishing to see more can find them—and buy prints—at his website: bruce@brucedale.com.

This book would not have been possible without the enthusiasm and support of Gillian MacKenzie, my friend and literary agent. She found a home for *Section 60* at Bloomsbury, where I am happy to be in the hands of the brilliant George Gibson, publishing director, and Jacqueline Johnson, an editor whose patience, grace, and steady judgment brought this book into print. Thanks also to Laura Phillips and Janet Biehl.

Finally, thanks and much love to my wife, Suzie, who keeps our ship moving forward.

APPENDIX

HOW TO HELP

A portion of the profits from this book will be donated to the Tragedy Assistance Program for Survivors (TAPS), a nonprofit organization with no government affiliation that has been helping the surviving friends and family of service members for twenty years—with a suicide prevention hotline, grief counseling programs, and workshops.

To learn more about TAPS or to
make a direct donation, call
(800) 959-TAPS
or visit their website:
http://taps.org/WaysToDonate

NOTES

1. The Longest War

1 Cdr. Kirk S. Lippold, interviewed by author, May 2, 2013; see also Cdr. Kirk S. Lippold, *Front Burner: Al Qaeda's Attack on the USS Cole* (New York: Public Affairs, 2012).

2 Lippold interview; Lippold, *Front Burner*.

3 Lippold interview; Lippold, *Front Burner*.

4 Katie Madden, fiancé of Pfc. Jared Vaquerano, e-mail to author, November 13, 2012.

5 Brittany Jacobs, interviewed by author, May 27, 2013; see also "A Day of Flags and Flowers," *New York Times*, May 28, 2013.

6 Anthony Coyer, interviewed by author, May 27, 2013.

7 Beth Belle, interviewed by author, May 8, 2012.

8 Paula Davis, interviewed by author, May 3, 2012.

9 Lance Cpl. Brandon Long, interviewed by author, April 3, 2012.

10 Master Sgt. David V. Hill, interviewed by author, May 19, 2013.

11 Ibid.; Bob Sipchen, "Days of Sadness and Joy," *Los Angeles Times*, November 17, 2006.

12 Hill interview.

2. RANGERS LEAD THE WAY

1 Joe and Rita Rippetoe, interviewed by author, October 9, 2012; Annie Gowen, "Father's Salute to a Son With 'a Big Heart,'" *Washington Post*, April 11, 2003; Lance Gay, "Arvada Ranger Is Laid to Rest at Arlington," *Rocky Mountain News*, April 11, 2003; Mike Soraghan, "Capt. Rippetoe's Last Request Honored," *Denver Post*, April 11, 2003.

2 As of July 15, 2013, 6,735 service members had died in the wars in Iraq (4,486) and Afghanistan (2,249); icasualties.org. Of those, 919 were buried in Section 60. Jennifer Lynch, public affairs office, Arlington National Cemetery, e-mail to author, May 20, 2013.

3 Rippetoe interview; funeral photographs, Rippetoe family papers.

4 Soraghan, "Capt. Rippetoe's Last Request"; Rippetoe interview.

5 Joe Rippetoe, "Words of Wisdom—Ranger Rip Senior," undated manuscript, Rippetoe family papers.

6 Rippetoe interview; Clay Latimer, "A Heart Laid Bare," *Rocky Mountain News*, April 3, 2004.

7 Rippetoe interview.

8 Ibid; Latimer, "Heart Laid Bare."

9 Chad Thibodeau, interviewed by author, March 11, 2013.

10 Latimer, "Heart Laid Bare."

11 Thibodeau interview.

12 Ibid.

13 Thibodeau recalled reports of the pregnant bomber but was not certain. "I may have been responsible for that idea getting out but in retrospect I don't think she was pregnant." Thibodeau interview.

14 Ibid.

15 Ibid. The official announcement, from U.S. Central Command, said that the car's driver and the woman were killed in the suicide bombing. Nicole Winfield, "Coloradan Among 3 GIs Slain in W. Iraq," Associated Press in *Denver Post*, April 6, 2003. Thibodeau recalled that there were three people in the car, including the older woman in the backseat. "She was having

some kind of medical complications," he said. Thibodeau interview.

16 Thibodeau interview.

17 Ibid.

18 Ibid. The explosion shattered Thibodeau's eye sockets, which were later reconstructed.

19 Winfield, "Coloradan Among 3 GIs."

20 Cheney made the "greeted as liberators" comment on March 16, 2003, as American forces mobilized for Iraq. "My belief is we will, in fact, be greeted as liberators," he told NBC's Tim Russert. Cheney's optimistic view of conditions in Iraq, which was shared by many in the neoconservative community, had been heavily influenced by Ahmed Chalabi, the Iraqi exile who saw himself as the logical replacement for Saddam Hussein. Chalabi exaggerated Saddam's possession of weapons of mass destruction and grossly underestimated the difficulties of occupation.

21 Thibodeau interview.

22 Ibid.; see also funeral photographs, Rippetoe family collection.

23 "A Hero's Welcome," *Gaithersburg Gazette*, April 16, 2003.

24 Soraghan, "Capt. Rippetoe's Last Request."

25 Latimer, "Heart Laid Bare."

26 "Rangers Dedicate Trophy to Fallen Comrade," *Bayonet* (Fort Benning, Georgia), April 16, 2004.

27 Ibid.; Rippetoe interview.

28 Thibodeau interview.

29 Ibid.

30 Philip L. Barbour, *The Three Worlds of Captain John Smith* (Boston: Houghton Mifflin, 1964), 209.

31 Robert E. Lee to Martha Custis "Markie" Williams, March 15, 1854, DeBuitts-Ely Collection, Library of Congress.

32 Robert M. Poole, *On Hallowed Ground: The Story of Arlington National Cemetery* (New York: Walker & Co., 2009), 58–99.

33 Edwina A. V. Avery, *The Arlington Experiment Farm of the United States Department of Agriculture: A Handbook of Information for Visitors* (Washington, D.C.: Bureau of Plant Industry, U.S. Department of Agriculture, 1928); "Arlington County in

Transition," Arlington Historical Society, http://www.arling tonhistory.org/learn-2/history-of-arlington-county/arlington-county-in-transition/.

34 "Planning Unit Picks Sites for Dormitories," *Washington Post*, April 17, 1942.

35 "Dormitories in Arlington Dedicated," *Washington Post*, October 10, 1943.

36 Jane Watson, "Critic Finds U.S. Housing Attractive," *Washington Post*, April 2, 1942.

37 "Death March Survivor Finds 'The Girl' Here," *Washington Post*, March 19, 1945.

38 Dorthea Andrews, "Arlington Farms Soon to Be a Memory to G-Girls," *Washington Post*, July 23, 1950; "Army Moves into G-Girls' Haven Today," *Washington Post*, September 1, 1950.

39 *Arlington National Cemetery: Master Plan* (Washington, D.C.: Rhodeside and Harwell, Inc., for the U.S. Army Corps of Engineers, 1998); Poole, *Hallowed Ground*, 209–29.

40 *Arlington National Cemetery*; Poole, *Hallowed Ground*.

41 *Arlington National Cemetery: Comprehensive Plan* (Washington, D.C.: Department of the Army, Office of the Chief of Support Services, 1967); *Arlington National Cemetery: Master Plan*, 1998.

42 Ami Neiberger-Miller, interviewed by author, April 25, April 30, 2012.

43 Author's personal observation.

44 Ibid.

45 "All night long the swift Achilles, lifting a two-handled cup, dipped wine from a golden bowl and poured it down on the ground and drenched the earth, calling out to the ghost of stricken, gaunt Patroclus." Homer, *The Iliad*, trans. Robert Fagles (New York: Viking, 1990), 566.

46 Mary Coyer, interviewed by author, May 26, 2013.

47 Ibid.

48 Roderick Gainer, interviewed by author, May 3, 2012.

49 Spec. Justin Allan Rollins, killed in Iraq in 2006, is buried in Grave No. 60-8502 with a baseball signed by David Ortiz, the Red Sox slugger. It was from the last game Rollins saw in Fenway Park.

50 Gainer interview.
51 Ibid.
52 Ibid.
53 Ibid.
54 Ibid.

3. Above and Beyond

1 Judy Meikle, interviewed by author, June 13, 2013; Meikle, e-mail to author, July 21, 2012.
2 As of August 4, 2013, 937 coalition service members had been killed in Helmand Province. The next highest number of fatalities, 535, came from neighboring Kandahar Province. "Operation Enduring Freedom," http://icasualties.org/OEF/ByProvince.aspx.
3 Jill Stephenson, CaringBridge website, July 15, 2009.
4 Ibid.; Stephenson, interviewed by author, May 31, 2013.
5 Ibid.
6 Stephenson interview, May 31, 2013.
7 Ibid.; Meikle interview.
8 Meikle interview.
9 Ibid.; Stephenson interview; Mark Berman, "The Heart of a Hero Beats On," *Washington Post*, August 8, 2009.
10 Berman, "Heart of a Hero."
11 Meikle interview.
12 Stephenson interview.
13 Ibid.
14 Meikle interview.
15 Ibid.
16 Ibid.
17 Ibid.
18 "Fallen Soldier's Heart Gives Mom New Strength and New Bond," KTSP.com, November 23, 2011, http://patdollard.com/2011/11/fallen-soldiers-heart-gives-mom-strength-and-new-bond-with-video/.

19 Simonides (556–468 B.C.) provided a famous epitaph for the Spartan warriors who died together, fighting to hold the line at Thermopylae: "O Stranger, send the news home to the people of Sparta that here we /Are laid to rest: the commands they gave us have been obeyed."

20 William Manchester, *Goodbye, Darkness: A Memoir of the Pacific War* (Boston: Little, Brown, 1980), 391.

21 Carrie McLeroy, "Second OIF Soldier to Receive Posthumous Medal of Honor," *Army News Service*, May 23, 2008.

22 Ibid.

23 Ibid.

24 Gregg Zoroya, "In Iraq, Coping After a Hero Dies Saving You," *USA Today*, September 27, 2007.

25 McLeroy, "Second OIF Soldier."

26 Ibid.

27 Ann Adams, interviewed by author, May 2 and 26, 2013.

28 Ibid.

29 Adams interview, May 26, 2013.

30 Bob Laylo, "Jim Thorpe Sergeant Drowns in Iraqi Canal," *Morning Call* (Allentown, Pa.), October 2, 2003.

31 Maj. John J. Marr, "Memorandum for Commanding General, 82nd Airborne Division, Fort Bragg, North Carolina: Report of AR 15-6 Investigation," October 23, 2003; hereafter AR 15-6 Report.

32 Sgt. First Class David R. Jaeckel, sworn statement, AR 15-6 Report.

33 Ibid.

34 Ibid.

35 Capt. Richard R. Balestri, sworn statement, AR 15-6 Report.

36 Adams interview, May 26, 2013.

37 Marr, "Memorandum for Commanding General."

38 Adams interview, May 26, 2013.

39 Ibid.

40 Ibid.

41 Terry Callen, comment at "Fallen Heroes of Operation Iraqi Freedom," http://www.fallenheroesmemorial.com/oif/profiles/baddickandrewjoseph.html.

42 Adams interview, May 27, 2013.

43 Ibid.; Adams interview, May 2, 2013.

44 Adams interview, May 27, 2013.

45 Cdr. James L. Caruso, "Final Autopsy Report," Armed Forces Institute of Pathology, Office of the Armed Forces Medical Examiner, October 2, 2003.

46 Michael Duke, sergeant major (retired), March 26, 2013, at "Fallen Heroes of Operation Iraqi Freedom," http://www.fall enheroesmemorial.com/oif/profiles/baddickandrewjoseph .html.

47 Sgt. Schelee K. Reece, March 26, 2013, at "Fallen Heroes of Operation Iraqi Freedom," http://www.fallenheroesmemorial .com/oif/profiles/baddickandrewjoseph.html.

48 Adams interview, May 27, 2013.

49 Ibid.; Alison Malachowski, interviewed by author, May 27, 2013.

50 Paula Davis, interviewed by author, May 27, 2013.

51 Ibid.

52 Thomas Heinlein, interviewed by author, May 27, 2013.

53 Gretel C. Kovach, "Deadly Helicopter Crash Caused by Bird," *San Diego Union-Tribune*, May 18, 2012.

54 Tristan Gale, interviewed by author, October 28, 2013.

4. From War to Peace

1 *Herodotus: The Histories*, trans. George Rawlinson (New York: Everyman's Library, 1997), 494–95.

2 Ibid., 599.

3 Steve Bentley, "A Short History of PTSD: From Thermopylae to Hue, Soldiers Have Always Had a Disturbing Reaction to War," *VVA Veteran*, January 1991; Matthew J. Friedman, "A Brief History of the PTSD Diagnosis," National Center for PTSD, U.S. Department of Veterans Affairs, December 20, 2011.

4 The most thorough study of the mental state of returning Iraq and Afghanistan war veterans, by the Rand Corporation, is out

of date. Published in 2008, the study relied upon direct, confidential reports from randomly selected veterans. Because of the stigma traditionally associated with mental illness in military culture, many of those affected do not report their condition, so official estimates of PTSD, TBI, and related injuries are almost certainly lower than the Rand benchmark. The author's estimate assumes that 18.5 percent of the 2.5 million deployed in recent wars meet the criteria for PTSD, TBI, or related illnesses, which could place the number of individuals in need of treatment at 462,000. T. Tanielian and L. H. Jaycox, eds., *Invisible Wounds of War: Psychological and Cognitive Injuries, Their Consequences, and Service to Assist Recovery* (Santa Monica, Calif.: Rand Corporation, MG-720-CCF, 2008).

5　Bonnie Carroll, remarks at the Army-Navy Club of Washington, D.C., April 3, 2013.

6　Liz Mocabee, interviewed by author, May 9, July 26, August 12, 2013; David V. Hill, interviewed by author, May 19, 2013.

7　Mocabee interview, May 9, 2013.

8　Hill interview.

9　Glenn Oliver, e-mail to author, May 9, 2013; interviewed by author, June 12, 2013.

10　Liz Mocabee, statement to Army Criminal Investigation Division, November 13, 2008, in Army ROI0095-2008-CID277-35088-5P, hereafter CID Report; interview, August 12, 2013.

11　Mocabee statement in CID Report.

12　Ibid.; Mocabee, e-mails to author, May 8, July 17, August 11, 2013.

13　Mocabee statement.

14　Mocabee interview, May 9, 2013.

15　Mocabee statement.

16　Mocabee interviews, May 9 and August 12, 2013.

17　Mocabee statement.

18　Ibid.

19　Ibid.; Mocabee interview, July 26, 2013.

20　CID Report.

21　Mocabee interview, May 9, 2013; Mocabee statement.

22 Mocabee statement.

23 Ibid.

24 Mocabee interview, May 9, 2013.

25 Ibid.

26 CID Report.

27 Mocabee interview, May 9, 2013.

28 Mocabee statement.

29 Liz Mocabee remarks, Sean Mocabee funeral service, Old Post Chapel, Fort Myer, Va., December 5, 2008.

30 Mocabee statement.

31 Mocabee to author, August 11, 2013.

32 CID Report.

33 Mocabee to author, August 11, 2013; Mocabee statement.

34 Mocabee statement; Mocabee interview, July 26, 2013.

35 CID Report. Note: Because of federal privacy laws, the names of Sean Mocabee's Army friends were redacted from the investigative report that followed his death; Mocabee to author, August 11, 2013.

36 Ibid.

37 Mocabee interview, May 9, 2013; CID Report.

38 Mocabee statement; Mocabee to author, July 17 and August 11, 2013.

39 CID Report; Hill interview.

40 Gwendolyn Haugen, former St. Louis County medical examiner, e-mail to author, April 2, 2013. Haugen, who has probed thousands of deaths, said that only about 30 percent of those who kill themselves leave suicide notes.

41 Mocabee to author, August 11, 2013.

42 Mocabee interview, May 9, 2013.

43 CID Report.

44 Ibid.

45 Capt. Rob Mocabee, remarks at funeral services for Sean Mocabee, Old Post Chapel, Fort Myer, Va., December 5, 2008. Note: The author was not present for Mocabee's service, but it was recorded on DVD by family members, who kindly shared copies, as well as extensive photographs of the church service and burial at Arlington.

46 Ibid.

47 Ibid.

48 Ibid.

49 Mocabee family DVD and photographs, December 5, 2008.

50 Mocabee statement.

51 Glenn G. Oliver, interviewed by author, June 12, 2013.

52 Hill interview.

53 Ibid.; the Ray Charles part of his name honors the singer, a favorite of Yost's mother.

54 Ibid.

55 Ibid.

56 Liz, Hayley, and Michael Mocabee, interviews by author, July 26, August 12, 2013; Sara Lloyd Truax, "Wounded Warriors: I've Got Your Back," *Santa Ynez Valley Journal*, November 1, 2012.

57 "MSGT Sean Mocabee," Facebook, https://www.facebook.com/pages/MSGT-Sean-Mocabee/38598178514.

58 Mocabee interview, August 12, 2013; Mocabee to author, August 11, 2013.

59 Mocabee interview, August 12, 2013.

60 Mocabee interview, May 9, 2013.

61 Christopher Munsey, "Frontlines of Care: Meet Four Psychologists Who Are Improving the Lives of Service Members, Veterans, and Families," *Monitor on Psychology* 42, no. 4 (April 2011).

62 Lt. Col. Pamela Novy, interviewed by author, December 12, 2012. Note: Lt. Col. Novy no longer takes patients to Section 60. In 2012 she transferred from the National Intrepid Center of Excellence in Bethesda, Md., to Elmendorf Air Force Base near Anchorage, Ak., where she continues to specialize in PTSD treatment.

63 Ibid.

64 Chase Martin, interviewed by author, May 15, 2013.

65 Ibid.

66 Ibid.

67 Ibid.

68 David Vergun, "Study Finds Soldiers' PTSD Diagnoses Accurate," *Army News Service*, March 8, 2013.

69 Fred Gusman, interviewed by author, June 16, 2010. See also Robert M. Poole, "The Pathway Home Makes Inroads in Treating PTSD," *Smithsonian*, September 2010.

70 Marine comrades told members of Hall's family that they had "found and fixed" the enemy who planted the IED, meaning they had killed him. Justin Hall, interviewed by author, April 13, 2013.

71 The quotes in this and the following paragraphs are from Becky Hall, Kevin Hall, Justin Hall, and Chaz Kane, interviewed by author, April 13, 2013.

72 Ibid.; Damien Cave, "Tracking a Marine Lost at Home," *New York Times*, March 31, 2008.

73 Kane interview.

74 Ibid.

75 Hall family interview; Cave, "Tracking a Marine Lost at Home."

76 Becky Hall interview.

77 Ibid.; Cave, "Tracking a Marine Lost at Home."

78 Ibid.

79 Ibid.

80 Becky Hall interview; "Medical Examiner Rules Eric Hall's Death 'Undetermined,'" *News and Tribune*, Jeffersonville, Indiana, March 28, 2008.

81 Becky Hall interview.

82 Kevin Hall interview.

5. Improvised Death

1 Alison Malachowski, interviewed by author, September 7, 2012.

2 Ibid. See also Brian Mockenhaupt, *The Living and the Dead: Not Even the Best Soldiers Can Always Save Their Friends* (Kindle Byliner Original, 2012).

3 Malachowski interview.

4 Ibid.

5 Mockenhaupt, *Living and Dead*.

6 Malachowski interview.

7 Staff Sgt. James M. Malachowski to Alison and James Malachowski, Sr., undated.

8 Staff Sgt. James M. Malachowski, e-mail to Lt. Brandy Malachowski, March 19, 2011.

9 Lt. Brandy Malachowski, promoted to captain in 2012, still serves in the Army.

10 James Malachowski to Brandy Malachowski.

11 Ibid.

12 Alison Malachowski interview; Mockenhaupt, *Living and Dead*, chap. 3.

13 Ibid.; Tom Whorl, interviewed by author, November 7, 2013.

14 Alison Malachowski interview; Mockenhaupt, *Living and Dead*, chap. 3; Whorl interview.

15 Mockenhaupt, *Living and Dead*, chap. 3; Whorl interview.

16 Ibid.

17 "Operation Enduring Freedom," http://icasualties.org/oef/.

18 William R. Levesque, "IEDs Continue to Kill and Maim U.S. Troops Despite Multibillion Dollar Effort," *Tampa Bay Times*, September 27, 2012.

19 Ibid.

20 "U.S. Military Struggles to Defeat IEDs," Associated Press, August 21, 2007; Peter Cary and Nancy Youssef, "JIEDDO: The Manhattan Project That Bombed," Center for Public Integrity, March 27, 2011; Capt. David F. Eisler, "Counter-IED Strategy in Modern War," *Military Review*, January–February 2012; Cary B. Russell, "Counter-Improvised Explosive Devices: Multiple DOD Organizations Are Developing Numerous Initiatives," U.S. Government Accountability Office, August 1, 2012; Andrew Cockburn, "Search and Destroy: The Pentagon's Losing Battle Against IEDs," *Harper's Magazine*, November 2011.

21 Rick Atkinson, "You Can't Armor Your Way Out of This Problem," *Washington Post*, October 2, 2007

22 Joint Improvised Explosive Device Defeat Organization, "Counter-Improvised Explosive Device Strategic Plan, 2012–2016," U.S. Department of Defense, January 1, 2012; Lt. Gen.

Michael D. Barbero, "The Unending War Against IEDs," *Washington Post*, May 19, 2013; Atkinson, "You Can't Armor"; Mockenhaupt, *Living and Dead*, chap. 3.

23 James Schear, statement, House Armed Services Committee, Subcommittee on Oversight and Investigations, U.S. House of Representatives, October 29, 2009.

24 Alison Malachowski, interviewed by author, September 7 and 21, 2012.

25 "Memorial Service for James M. Malachowski, Staff Sergeant, U.S. Marine Corps, April 7, 2011," DVD (Falls Church, Va.: Ventures in Video, 2011), hereafter "Memorial Service DVD."

26 Ibid.

27 Ibid.

28 Ibid.

29 Ibid.

30 Malachowski interview, September 21, 2012; Alison Malachowski, e-mail to author, October 11, 2013; Tom Whorl, e-mail to author, November 11, 2013.

31 Staff Sgt. James M. Malachowski, e-mail to Lt. Brandy Malachowski, March 19, 2011.

32 Memorial Service DVD.

33 Ibid.; Alison Malachowski, e-mail to author, October 6, 2013.

34 Memorial Service DVD.

35 Malachowski interviews, September 7 and 21, 2012; Mockenhaupt, *Living and Dead*, chap. 5.

36 Ami Neiberger-Miller, interviewed by author, May 2, 2013; Malachowski interviews, September 7 and 21, 2012.

37 Ibid.; Ami Neiberger-Miller, interviewed by author, April 30, 2012, and May 2, 2013.

38 Darcie Sims, remarks in TAPS workshop, "Surviving the Death of an Adult Child," May 25, 2013.

39 Malachowski interviews, September 7 and 21, 2012.

40 Malachowski interview, September 7, 2012.

41 Ibid.; Mockenhaupt, *Living and Dead*, chap. 5.

42 Malachowski interviews, September 7 and 21, 2012.

43 Malachowski interview, September 21, 2012.

44 Ibid.

45 Whorl interview; Mockenhaupt, *Living and Dead*, chap. 5.

46 Tom Whorl, comments written on Jimmy Malachowski's laptop, May 26, 2011. The laptop was later shipped to Alison Malachowski, who shared it with the author. "I didn't do anything to clean it up," she said. "It still has the grit from Afghanistan in it." Malachowski interview, September 21, 2012.

47 Mockenhaupt, *Living and Dead*, chap. 5. The description of events leading to Whorl's attempted suicide and his recovery comes from Mockenhaupt's book. "He got it right," Whorl interview.

48 Mockenhaupt, *Living and Dead*, chap. 5.

49 Whorl interview.

50 Malachowski interviews, September 7 and 21, 2012.

51 Ibid.

52 Malachowski interview, May 27, 2013.

53 Author's personal observation.

54 Ami Neiberger-Miller, interviewed by author, August 12, 2013.

55 Alison Malachowski, interviewed by author, July 26, 2013.

56 Ibid.

57 Greg Jaffe, "Cleanup in Arlington National Cemetery's Section 60 Upsets Families of War Dead," *Washington Post*, October 1, 2013.

58 Jennifer Lynch, e-mail to author, August 5, 2013.

59 Andrew Tilghman, "Arlington's Sweep of Gravesite Mementoes Distresses Families of Fallen," *Marine Corps Times*, October 10, 2013.

60 Ami Neiberger-Miller, interviewed by author, October 7, 2013; Ami Neiberger-Miller, e-mail to author, October 11, 2013; Robin Chapman Stacey, "Let Arlington's Dead Live a Little Longer," *Washington Post* op-ed, October 6, 2013; "Arlington Cemetery Will Allow Small Mementoes," Associated Press, October 16, 2013.

61 Confidential interview by author, January 8, 2014.

62 Paula Davis, interviewed by author, May 6, 2013, and August 13, 2013.

6. Friendly Fire

1 David H. Sharrett, interviewed by author, April 24, 2013.

2 David H. Sharrett and James Gordon Meek, *Fallen Eagles: A Father's Wartime Fight for Justice*, unpublished manuscript, 20–21. The following account of the day Sharrett first learned of his son's death comes largely from *Fallen Eagles*, supplemented by the Sharrett interview.

3 Sharrett and Meek, *Fallen Eagles*; Sharrett interview.

4 Sharrett and Meek, *Fallen Eagles*, 39–40; see also Tom Jackman, "David Sharrett's Family Still Wants Justice for Friendly Fire Death in Iraq," *Washington Post*, February 26, 2012.

5 Brig. Gen. David J. Bishop, "Unclassified Informal Army Regulation 15-6 Investigation—Operation Hood Harvest," March 31, 2011; Sharrett and Meek, *Fallen Eagles*, 37–55; Jackman, "David Sharrett's Family."

6 Ibid.

7 "DOD Identifies Army Casualties," January 17, 2008.

8 Sharrett and Meek, *Fallen Eagles*, 24.

9 Tillman was posthumously promoted from specialist to corporal in 2004 and awarded the Silver Star for gallantry.

10 Jon Krakauer, *Where Men Win Glory: The Odyssey of Pat Tillman* (New York: Doubleday, 2009).

11 Lt. Cdr. Mark Shelly, "Autopsy Examination Report," Armed Forces Institute of Pathology, Office of the Armed Forces Medical Examiner, January 28, 2008.

12 Jackman, "David Sharrett's Family"; Sharrett and Meek, *Fallen Eagles*, 26–28.

13 The following account is drawn from Sharrett and Meek, *Fallen Eagles*, 27–30.

14 Ibid., 29–30. In later investigations, McCarthy was adamant that he never denied Sharrett's death by friendly fire in the pivotal January 25, 2008, telephone call to David Sharrett Senior. McCarthy said he was responding to a suggestion that Sharrett had been killed by helicopter fire—a suggestion the elder Sharrett never raised. McCarthy maintained that the family's confusion about Sharrett's death was the result of

misunderstanding. This interpretation, ultimately endorsed by the Army's chief investigator, is not supported by McCarthy's written description of the firefight, conveyed to Sharrett by e-mail on January 27, 2008.

15 Lt. Col. Robert H. McCarthy III, e-mail to David Sharrett, January 27, 2008; see also Bishop, "Unclassified Informal Army Regulation 15-6 Investigation."

16 Kenneth K. Steinwig, "Dealing Realistically with Fratricide," *Parameters*, Strategic Studies Institute, U.S. Army War College, Spring 1995.

17 Julian Humphreys, "The Fog of War," Historyextra.com, *BBC History*, April 15, 2011, http://www.historyextra.com/blog/fog-war.

18 Fred Anderson, ed., *George Washington Remembers: Reflections on the French and Indian War* (Lanham, Md.: Rowman & Littlefield, 2004), 167.

19 Catherine M. Webb and Kate J. Hewett, "An Analysis of U.S. Army Fratricide Incidents during the Global War on Terror (11 September 2001 to 31 March 2008)," U.S. Army Aeromedical Research Laboratory, Warfighter Performance and Health Division, March 2010.

20 Krakauer, *Where Men Win Glory*, 343. Krakauer's 40 percent figure, for which he cites no source, seems so high as to strain credulity.

21 Sharrett and Meek, *Fallen Eagles*, 33–34.

22 Ibid.

23 Ibid.

24 David H. Sharrett, interviewed by Brig. Gen. David J. Bishop, March 3, 2011.

25 David H. Sharrett, "We Are Looking for Accountability," undated manuscript in David H. Sharrett papers.

26 Maj. Rob Young, in AR 15-6 Report, February 22, 2008.

27 Brig. Gen. Steven J. Townsend, e-mail to Maj. Gen. Jeffrey J. Schloesser and others, April 2, 2009.

28 Sharrett and Meek, *Fallen Eagles*, 59.

29 Ibid.

30 Ibid.; see also Young, in AR 15-6 Report.

31 Sharrett and Meek, *Fallen Eagles*, 59.

32 Lt. Timothy R. Hanson, interviewed by Brig. Gen. David J. Bishop, February 25, 2011.

33 Brig. Gen. David J. Bishop, "Memorandum for Director of the Army Staff," March 31, 2011.

34 Maj. Timothy Brumfiel, interviewed by Brig. Gen. David J. Bishop, March 4, 2011.

35 Jackman, "David Sharrett's Family."

36 Col. Scott McBride, in Sharrett and Meek, *Fallen Eagles*, 43.

37 Ibid.

38 Jackman, "David Sharrett's Family."

39 Sharrett and Meek, "Firefight Tick-Tock," timetable of Bichigan firefight, *Fallen Eagles*.

40 Sharrett and Meek, *Fallen Eagles*, 72.

41 Lt. Timothy R. Hanson, sworn statements, January 19 and 25, 2008.

42 Bishop memorandum, March 31, 2011.

43 Ibid.

44 "Colonel McBride wrote that letter of reprimand to pacify me," Sharrett said when interviewed by Brig. Gen. David J. Bishop on March 3, 2011. "There was never an LOR [Letter of Reprimand] until I asked for it—insisted on it—demanded it because I had a very frank conversation with him."

45 Col. Michael S. McBride, "Memorandum for 1LT Timothy R. Hanson," October 22, 2008.

46 Jackman, "David Sharrett's Family."

47 Permanent Order 087-056F, Department of the Army, Combat Infantryman Badge, March 27, 2008; Joe Gould, "Army Probes CIB Given to Lt. Who Shot Soldier," *Army Times*, May 7, 2012.

48 Sharrett interview by Bishop.

49 Sharrett and Meek, *Fallen Eagles*, 62.

50 Ibid.

51 Townsend to Schloesser and others, April 2, 2009.

52 Sharrett and Meek, *Fallen Eagles*, 67.

53 Sharrett interview by author.

54 Sharrett and Meek, *Fallen Eagles*, 65.

55 Sharrett interview by author.

56 Sharrett and Meek, *Fallen Eagles*, 62.

57 James Gordon Meek, "Army Lied About How My Son Died in Iraq," *New York Daily News*, April 1, 2009; Joe Gould, "Army to Take New Look at Friendly Fire Death," *Army Times*, March 20, 2011; Corey Flintoff, "Soldiers' Families Haunted By Friendly Fire," National Public Radio, April 1, 2009.

58 Jackman, "David Sharrett's Family"; Jackman's video, "Anatomy of a Friendly Fire Incident: Inside Operation Hood Harvest," is at http://www.liveleak.com/view?i=103_1361559990.

59 David H. Sharrett, letter to Gen. George W. Casey, Jr., December 18, 2009.

60 Ibid.

61 Bishop memorandum, March 31, 2011.

62 Ibid.

63 Ibid.

64 Ibid.

65 Ibid.

66 Ibid.

67 We know of Hanson's GOMOR not because it was announced but because it was inadvertently mentioned in a note from the Senior Army Decorations Board, which cited the reprimand as its reason for stripping Hanson's Combat Infantryman's Badge (CIB) "based on GOMOR received for same action that supported the C.I.B." Lt. Col. Ralph N. Perkins IV, "Memorandum Thru Commander, 84th Training Command, Fort Knox, KY," June 14, 2012.

68 Hanson's only known comment was made to Tom Jackman, the dogged *Washington Post* reporter who tracked Hanson to Janesville, Wis., where he resettled with his wife and family. "I've always wanted to apologize to the Sharretts," Hanson told Jackman, in "David Sharrett's Family." "Eventually, I'd like to do it in person. I do want to say I'm sorry." For his part, Sharrett said his family would still welcome such a visit. "We're still waiting," he said, in interview by author, April 24, 2013.

69 David Sharrett, undated notes of June 29, 2012, telephone conversation with Gordon I. Peterson, military legislative

assistant to then-senator Jim Webb of Virginia. See also Joe Gould, "Army Probes CIB Given to Lt. Who Shot Soldier," *Army Times*, April 27, 2012.

70 Sharrett interview by author; Sharrett and Meek, *Fallen Eagles*, 79.

7. THE LONG WAY HOME

1 First Sgt. Robert A. Durbin, interviewed by author, May 30, 2013.

2 "Soldier Missing from Korean War Identified," U.S. Department of Defense, Office of the Assistant Secretary of Defense (Public Affairs), June 13, 2011.

3 Although President Harry S. Truman ordered desegregation of the armed forces in July 1948, it took another five years for his directive to take effect. Many of those who served in Korea, including A. V. Scott, fought in all-black units. Perhaps the best known was Sgt. Charles Rangel of New York, who earned the Bronze Star for heroism, returned to the United States, ran for Congress from Harlem, and continues to serve New York's Thirteenth Congressional District.

4 Mike Wilkinson, "Remains of Detroit Soldier Killed in Korean War Identified," *Detroit News*, June 14, 2011.

5 In wars previous to Korea, the dead were gathered in and shipped home at the end of hostilities for families requesting repatriation. Because of advances in refrigeration and faster transportation times, the Korean conflict became the first war in which the war dead came home concurrently. This innovation caused political headaches in later wars, when the long lines of flag-draped caskets arriving at Dover Air Force Base revealed the human cost of the fighting in Vietnam, Iraq, and Afghanistan.

6 Figures on missing service members come from the Joint POW/MIA Accounting Command (JPAC), Hickam Air Force Base, Hawaii, http://www.jpac.pacom.mil/Portals/64/

Documents/Fact%20Sheets/Missing%20Persons.pdf;   see also Robert M. Poole, "Lost Over Laos," *Smithsonian*, August 2006.

7 William Douglas Lansford, "Clyde Thomason: The Forgotten Hero," *Leatherneck*, August 2013, September 2013; Maj. Jon T. Hoffman, "From Makin to Bougainville: Marine Raiders in the Pacific War," Marine Corps Historical Center, Washington, D.C., 1995.

8 Lansford, "Clyde Thomason"; Hoffman, "From Makin to Bougainville."

9 Ibid.

10 Ibid.

11 Lansford, "Clyde Thomason."

12 Ibid.; Hoffman, "From Makin to Bougainville."

13 Lansford, "Clyde Thomason."

14 Lt. W. S. LeFrancois, "We Mopped Up Makin Island," *Saturday Evening Post*, December 4 and 11, 1943.

15 Lt. Wilfred S. LeFrancois, letter to Mrs. C. A. Thomason, May 17, 1943.

16 Arlo Wagner, "13 Marines Put in Hallowed Ground 59 Years to Day After Death in Pacific," *Washington Times*, August 18, 2001.

17 Lansford, "Clyde Thomason"; Hoffman, "From Makin to Bougainville."

18 At this writing, the remains of the beheaded Marines have not been found, although JPAC has launched preliminary inquiries on Kwajalein Island, the last known location for the nine Marines. The officer who ordered their execution, Japanese Adm. Kose Abe, commander of the Marshall Islands, was convicted of war crimes and hanged after the end of World War II.

19 Lansford, "Clyde Thomason"; Hoffman, "From Makin to Bougainville."

20 President Roosevelt, playing the xenophobic card with characteristic flair, recoiled when Lt. Gen. Thomas Holcomb, the Marine commandant, unfurled the captured flag for him in Washington a month after the raid. "I don't think I want to

touch it," he said, acting as if the banner were contaminated. FDR asked Holcomb to put the flag in the Marine Corps archives. Associated Press, "F.D.R. Accepts New U.S. Flag, Refuses to Touch Jap Emblem," *Atlanta Constitution*, September 18, 1942.

21 Lansford, "Clyde Thomason"; Hoffman, "From Makin to Bougainville."

22 Ibid.

23 President Franklin D. Roosevelt, Medal of Honor citation, January 16, 1943.

24 Al Sharp, "Atlanta Marine Awarded Medal for Heroism in Makin," *Atlanta Constitution*, January 21, 1943.

25 Capt. C. P. Lancaster, U.S. Marine Corps, to Mrs. Amy M. Thomason, October 3, 1942.

26 Lt. Col. Jack Lewis, "A Search for Shadows: Nearly Six Decades After the Raid, the Search Goes On for the Graves of the Makin Atoll Casualties," *Leatherneck*, December 1999.

27 Capt. Edwin C. Clarke, U.S. Marine Corps, to Mrs. Amy Thomason, July 16, 1946.

28 Hugh M. Thomason, letter to Bill Paupe, Honorary Consul, Republic of Kiribati, Honolulu, Hawaii, July 31, 1992.

29 Karel Margry, "Recovery of Missing Makin Raiders," *After the Battle*, no. 108 (n.d.).

30 "Makin Atoll Recovery Mission Photos," http.//www.cilhi .army.mil/Makinrecpics.html.

31 Col. David J. Pagano, "Search and Recovery Report 1999/ CIL/076, A Mass Grave Site Associated with KIR-1, Tabonibwa Ward, Butaritari, Republic of Kiribati, 30 November through 17 December 1999," April 4, 2000.

32 Ibid.

33 Sgt. Kane Walsh, "Missing WW2 Marines' Remains Repatriated," *Marine Corps News*, December 17, 1999.

34 Pagano, "Search and Recovery Report."

35 James R. Carroll, "Marine Raiders Killed in WWII Laid to Rest," *Louisville Courier-Journal*, August 18, 2001.

36 William Cole, "13 Marine Raiders to Be Buried Together at Arlington," *Honolulu Advertiser*, August 14, 2001.

37 Carroll, "Marine Raiders."

38 Hugh M. Thomason, interviewed by author, July 16, 2012.

39 Accounting for missing service members from the Vietnam War, like other aspects of that conflict, has been the subject of controversy. The most generally agreed-upon figures are as follows: 2,550 were killed in action (1,200) or died as POWs (1,350) during the war. Of this number, more than 900 have been recovered, identified, and repatriated since the end of hostilities, according to the Defense Department's POW/Missing Personnel Office. The 672 POWs who survived the war and returned to the United States in Operation Homecoming (February–April 1973) came from prisons in North Vietnam (591), Vietcong jails in South Vietnam (69), Laos (9), and China (3).

40 Colleen Shine, interviewed by author, May 9, 2013.

41 Ibid.

42 Wyatt Olson, "50 Years After Start of Vietnam War, US Presses to Recover Remains," *Stars and Stripes*, May 19, 2012.

43 Shine interview.

44 It is remarkable that Anthony Shine developed the dexterity and strength to fly jets as an adult. Infected with polio at age eleven, he lay motionless in bed for months, lost the use of both hands, and was so weak that he could not pick up a pencil with either one. He had muscle transplants to restore the use of his badly atrophied left hand, which remained smaller than his right one for the rest of his life. But with characteristic doggedness and discipline, he threw himself into physical therapy, learned to walk and use his hands again, and grew to an imposing six foot, 230-pound hulk. He qualified as a starting player for Colgate University's football team. He not only passed the strict physical requirements for the Air Force but served as a flight instructor before going to Vietnam. Anthony, Colleen, Shannon, and Bomette "Bonnie" Shine, "Overcoming Incredible Odds," in Jan Scruggs, comp., *Dreams Unfulfilled: Stories of the Men and Women on the Vietnam Veterans Memorial* (Vietnam Veterans Memorial Fund, 2010).

45 Capt. Anthony C. Shine, letter to Colleen Shine, November 26, 1972.

46 Colleen Shine interview.

47 Ibid.

48 Jennifer McFarland Flint, "What Remains: A Vietnam Pilot's Daughter and Her Fight For Answers," *Wellesley*, Winter 2013.

49 Ibid.

50 Colleen Shine, "Keeping the Faith: Unraveling the Disappearance of Anthony Shine: A Family's Relentless Pursuit of the Truth," *Ghost Wings*, no. 8 (2002).

51 Flint, "What Remains."

52 Ibid.; see also Shine, "Keeping the Faith."

53 Flint, "What Remains."

54 Col. Alexander P. Shine, "Remarks at Funeral of Lt. Col. Anthony Shine, USAF," October 11, 1996.

55 Colleen Shine interview.

56 Ibid.

57 Wil S. Hylton, "The Search for the Lost Marines of Tarawa," *New York Times Magazine*, November 20, 2013.

58 Colleen Shine interview.

8. FINAL HONORS

1 Service members qualify for burial at Arlington National Cemetery if they meet one of these criteria: they died on active duty; they had at least twenty years of active service; they served on active reserve and qualified for pay upon retirement; they were retired for disability; they were honorably discharged with a disability of 30 percent or greater before October 1, 1949; they received the Medal of Honor, Distinguished Service Cross, the Air Force Cross, the Navy Cross, the Distinguished Service Medal, the Silver Star, or the Purple Heart; they were prisoners of war; they were the spouses or unmarried minors of a qualifying service member. Any former president of the United States also qualifies for burial, as do former armed forces members

who served on active duty and held elective office in the federal government or were a Supreme Court justice. In addition, honorably discharged veterans qualify for inurnment in Arlington's columbarium, which is set aside for cremated remains.

2 Staff Sgt. T. J. Goodman, interviewed by author, October 4, 2012.

3 Technically, the horses are gray or dark bay, not white or black. Soldiers in the Caisson Platoon know this very well. Their reference to "white team" and "black team" is a shorthand used for convenience, which the author follows here.

4 Anonymous soldier, interviewed by author.

5 Quotes in this and the next paragraphs are from Staff Sgt. William Whitley, interviewed by author, August 21, 2012.

6 Sgt. Jake France, interviewed by author, August 22, 2012. Because the triple volley is fired by seven weapons, this part of a funeral service is often mistaken for a twenty-one-gun salute, an honor reserved for the president of the United States or the nation itself, usually fired with 75-millimeter cannons.

7 U.S. Department of Veterans Affairs, http://www.cem.va.gov/ hmm/emblems.asp. The Wiccan name is rooted in Old English, in which the noun *wicca* meant "witch." Among Wiccans in the United States, the emphasis is on nature worship and benign magic. Satanic cults have used an inverted version of the pentacle as the "devil's star," in which an arm of the star points below. Those approved for Arlington and other national cemeteries have the single arm pointing up.

8 Ibid.

9 Louis Sahagun, "Wiccans Want Their Star on Vets' Graves," *Los Angeles Times*, October 14, 2006; "Veterans Win Right to Post Religious Symbol on Headstones," Press Release, American Civil Liberties Union, April 23, 2007.

10 Thomas Heinlein, interviewed by author, May 26, 2013.

11 Staff Sgt. Alfredo Caballero, interviewed by author, April 19, 2013.

12 Confidential statement of a father whose son was killed in Iraq. He made his comments to an army officer conducting an investigation of the soldier's death.

13 Mother of a Marine killed in Afghanistan, e-mail to author, December 2, 2013. Names withheld at mother's request.

14 Master Sgt. Christopher D. Albright, interviewed by author, February 15 and September 6, 2013.

15 Lt. Jonathan Bush, interviewed by author, December 6, 2012.

16 Lance Cpl. Ruben Franco, interviewed by author, March 19, 2013.

17 Cpl. Brian Bell, interviewed by author, March 19, 2013.

18 Lance Cpl. James Hamby, interviewed by author, March 19, 2013.

19 Lance Cpl. Gary Miller, interviewed by author, March 19, 2013.

20 Arlington Ladies represent the Army, Navy, Air Force, and Coast Guard for funeral services—but not the Marine Corps, which prefers to send uniformed members of its service to console the bereaved before, during, and after ceremonies at Arlington. "We take care of our own people," said Master Sgt. William J. Dixon, who represented the commandant at hundreds of funerals before retiring a few years ago.

21 Jean Anderegg, interviewed by author, December 18, 2012.

22 Staff Sgt. Jennifer Powell, interviewed by author, May 3, 2013.

23 Oriana Pawlyk, "AF Female Body Bearer Talks Teamwork, Days at Arlington," *Marine Corps Times*, May 26, 2013.

AFTERWORD

1 Staff Sgt. John McDermott and Staff Sgt. Michael Drake, interviewed by author, April 12, 2013.

INDEX